GLEN LOATES

A BRUSH WITH LIFE

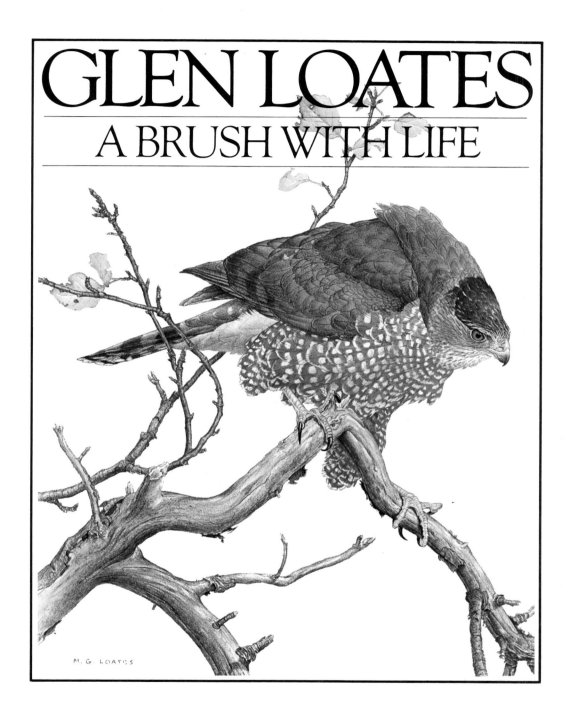

M. G. LOATES

GLEN LOATES

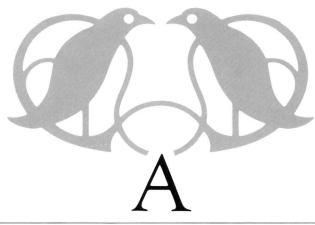

A
BRUSH
WITH
LIFE

TEXT BY GLEN WARNER
PRENTICE-HALL CANADA INC., SCARBOROUGH, ONTARIO

Published in Canada by Prentice-Hall Canada Inc.
1870 Birchmound Road, Scarborough, Ontario M1P 2J7

First Edition 1984

Canadian Cataloguing in Publication Data

Warner, Glen, 1947 –
  Glen Loates: A brush with life
  ISBN 0-13-357061-4
1. Loates, Glen. 2. Animal painters – Canada –
Biography 3. Animals in art. I. Loates, Glen. II. Title.
QH46 5W37   759.11   C83-098063-6

The publisher would like to thank the following people whose encouragement, support, and co-operation helped make this book possible:

The collectors
Wallace Matheson
Jan Whitford
Rand Paterson
Elynor Kagan
Alexander Schaeffer
Marten DeVries
Michael Thompson

Typography by Word for Word Inc.

Printed and bound in Belgium by Brepols

Photo credits:
Page 18: A.A. Loates
Page 42: Maclean's Magazine
Page 81: John Franks
Page 118: W.A. Loates
Page 176: Courtesy The White House, Washington D.C.

Photographic source references:
S. Dalton
H.M. Halliday
E. Muybridge
E. Hosking

Uncaptioned illustrations:
Page 1/Cooper's Hawk
Pages 2, 3/Golden Eagle
Page 5/Raccoon Family
Pages 6, 7/Milkweed Odyssey
Pages 8, 9/Barn Swallows
Page 10/Apple Tree
Page 12/Berries
Pages 14, 15/Timber Wolves
Page 16/Cardinals

For many
non-migrant birds,
the ripening of seed and berry crops
in the late summer and autumn
assures them a supply of food
for the winter months.

I DEDICATE
THIS VOLUME
TO MY WIFE
SALLY
AND MY SONS
CHRISTOPHER
AND
MICHAEL

CONTENTS

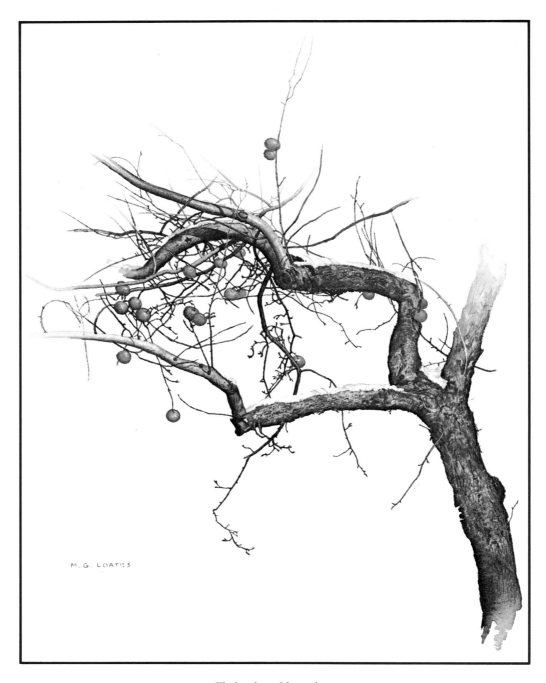

M.G. LOATES

*The late fruit of the apple tree
can be a winter feast for such permanent residents
as the grosbeaks.*

FOREWORD

IF IMITATION IS INDEED THE SINCEREST FORM OF FLATTERY, NO OTHER CONTEMPORARY WILDLIFE ARTIST HAS BEEN PAID A GREATER TRIBUTE BY HIS peers than has Glen Loates. Working alone, formulating his unique vision through the most intensive and rigorous discipline, he established his reputation well before nature painting began to enjoy its current surge in popularity. His art, in all its scope and detail, has remained unswayed by momentary trends. Rather, it was Loates who set the trends, with self-imposed standards of excellence others could only strive to equal.

You hold the results in your hands—but the paintings reproduced here constitute something of an interim report. Loates has not yet reached the height of his powers, even though a lifetime's honors have already come his way. By the age of 20 he was recognized both at home and abroad. His paintings hang today in public and private collections the world over, and he has been critically acclaimed for showings in galleries and museums across Canada, the United States and Europe. Two earlier books, *The Art of Glen Loates* and *Birds of North America*, achieved instant best-seller status. Reproductions and limited edition prints of his work are eagerly sought by enthusiastic purchasers. He has been the subject of several television and motion picture documentaries. And in December 1982, he personally presented President Reagan with a majestic portrait entitled *The Bald Eagle*—a gift from the Canadian people, commemorating the 200th anniversary of the eagle's designation as official symbol of the United States of America.

How did all this come about? Glen Loates is undoubtedly a consummate draftsman, capable of rendering virtually any species in any pose he wishes. His works display an almost deceptive ease, recalling one definition of genius—the ability to do repeatedly and without apparent effort what other people cannot do at all. But behind each painting lies a wealth of heightened sensitivity and trained perception. Maturity, selectivity and control have come gradually, through time. Raw gifts are not sufficient, and Loates has honed and refined his talents for two decades and more.

Like many people, I first became aware of Glen Loates' art in the pages of *The Canadian*, a mass-circulation magazine which published numerous collections of his nature paintings between 1965 and 1971. I well recall the pleasure of opening an issue containing his latest portfolio, and marveling at his wonderfully life-like portraits of creatures great and small. Then, as now, his subjects ranged from the most delicate wildflowers to ferocious predators. His work, even in those early days, held an exceptionally powerful appeal, providing confirmed city-dwellers with a window into the world we would never ourselves experience. Glen Loates seemed to reach out to everyone, children and connoisseurs alike. The verdict was immediate and unequivocal: Loates had touched us all, and we responded from the heart.

How could we have done otherwise? Loates' animals—rendered by a man who'd gone among them, seen them in the flesh, learned their every contour, their lightning movements and subtle colorations —came leaping out at us from the printed page. Loates glories in confrontation and interaction, those dramatic encounters that entail something totally new—some never-to-be-repeated instant, pulsing with life, illuminated for the first time. Perhaps this is what one critic meant when he remarked that Loates "sees nature with eyes that retain the exuberance of youth."

Exuberance, to be sure, but scarcely innocence. Loates is not a sentimentalist, and his concerns are founded in clear and present perils. The daily news reports contain a litany of ecological doom: acid rain, endangered species, ravaged wilderness areas. On impulse, we respond—but do we truly understand? Perhaps not. But Glen Loates *does* and, through his art, arouses in us a more complete sense of impending loss, a renewed commitment to preserve and protect our increasingly threatened environment.

Glen Loates succeeds in doing all this and more—but even his most devoted admirers may fail to realize what a difficult task he undertakes. The portraits in this volume appear in literal perfection, but how was each created? I hope that *A Brush With Life* will tell you how, fostering in the process a deeper appreciation of Loates' accomplishments.

Consider for a moment that Loates must assume at once three very different roles: the technician, the designer and the

"As the days of summer begin to shorten the evenings become cooler, clouds of insects fill the air and branches become laden with berries and seeds."

anatomist. Or, in his words, he must present in a single image "skill, ideas and knowledge." The pitfalls are many and varied. A superbly rendered animal, set in a pleasing posture, might in fact violate nature by its unrealistic activity. A painting, though both faithful in its depiction of an animal's stance and beautifully drawn, might be inadequately conceived, and thus a lesser work of art. Loates accepts a triple challenge each time he sets brush to paper. Add to this the fact that as he matures, he seems purposely to court extraordinary problems, to take extreme risks with bravura works that tax his abilities. The results are not mere "scientific studies," or (that supreme backhanded compliment) works of "photographic accuracy." They are art, and art of the highest order.

It has been said that every painting, in some way, becomes a self-portrait of its creator. Glen Loates' passionate involvement with the natural world is plain to see—an impression I have been privileged to confirm. At our initial meetings, I discovered a modest, softspoken man who remains reluctant to discuss his professional success, but who reveals an encyclopedic knowledge of both art and nature in all their forms. I was fortunate enough to accompany him on numerous sketching expeditions, and spent countless hours in his studio, listening and watching while he created many of the paintings reproduced in this book. Through others, I became aware of his extreme generosity—the largely unpublicized donation of his time, and frequently his art, that benefits any number of environmental groups and causes. I am deeply grateful for the many hours he made available to me, the care he took to explain and demonstrate his highly technical working methods.

A Brush With Life is a tribute to Glen Loates' most recent achievements—an important compilation of work produced between 1977 and 1984. In addition, it traces his development from rough boyhood sketches to his present style.

In one sense, Loates' art stands alone, a statement unto itself. But, not unnaturally, we wish to know more, see more. As readers and viewers, we demand a fuller portrait. This is what *A Brush With Life* attempts to provide—a definitive exploration of Glen Loates' profound love of nature, the wellspring of his creativity and unfailing inspiration for his art.

Glen Warner
Toronto, Ontario
1984

The timber wolf is a savage, powerful killer.
It has been one of the most feared and hated animals in the white man's world.
Yet there is no kinder and more devoted mate in the wild fauna
of North America. A tender, conscientious father, he labors long hours to care for his
offspring. Usually a sociable fellow, he prefers to hunt with his relatives
and friends than to go alone. The bloodthirsty mother is affectionate and big hearted
and has been said to have added wolf orphans to her own brood.
The hero and heroine, the villain and villainess of folklore.
Occasionally the wolf stalks or ambushes large prey, but it runs down most deer,
caribou, bighorn, elk, moose and antelope in open chase. It is easier
if members of a pack can work in relays, but a lone wolf is not hopelessly handicapped.
The wolf selects a band and chases it for a mile or two.
If a weakling does not drop behind, the wolf turns away and tests another group.
Sometimes many miles are run before a crippled caribou cannot keep
up with its companions. Swinging along at a swift gallop, the wolf slowly closes the gap
between him and his prey for the kill.

INTRODUCTION

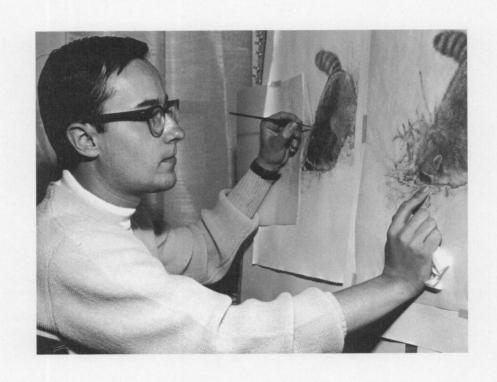

THE EARLY YEARS

THE ART PRACTICED SO MAGNIFICENTLY BY GLEN LOATES BENEFITS FROM A RICH HERITAGE DATING BACK TO PREHISTORIC TIMES. NATURE'S BEAUTY HAS been a source of artistic inspiration since cave dwellers first sketched bison, horses and deer in the caves of Lascaux and Altamira over 20 000 years ago.

Indeed, *every* age has prompted artists and artisans to embrace nature in painting and sculpture. The Egyptians embellished their public buildings, tombs and pottery with representations of cats, falcons, eagles and lions, as did the ancient Greeks and Romans. Affection and admiration for animals is evident in illuminated manuscripts of the Middle Ages, and in paintings and drawings of the Renaissance period—the works of Leonardo da Vinci, Michelangelo and Albrecht Dürer. Animals appear as decorative elements in their larger compositions, as well as in detailed, though sometimes fanciful, sketches and studies.

In the nineteenth century, however, artists began to create wildlife art as we know it today—paintings in which animals are depicted as principal subjects in their natural habitats. Three artists, John James Audubon (1785-1851), Louis Agassiz Fuertes (1874-1927) and Archibald Thorburn (1860-1935) raised animal art to new levels of excellence and public acceptance. Their paintings exerted such a profound effect on the young Glen Loates that no study of his art would be complete without an examination of the manner and style in which they worked.

In 1827, Audubon published the first set of engravings in his magnificent *Birds of America* collection—an attempt to illustrate all then-known species life-size in realistic settings. A naturalist by profession, he observed his subjects in their proper habitats—but, lacking photographic equipment and a means of refrigeration, he was forced to kill many of his specimens. Audubon wired birds in representative poses and painted them with extreme speed before decomposition set in. Contemporary critics would fault him for unnatural stiffness, and for his habit of distorting large subjects to make them fit a stan-

To see a World in a grain of sand,
And a Heaven in a wild flower,
Hold Infinity in the palm of your hand,
And Eternity in an hour.
William Blake

dard sheet size, but Loates disagrees, insisting that Audubon was greatly ahead of his time. Whatever one's point of view, Audubon's impact cannot be overstated. When Glen Loates was ten years old, he was given a book of Audubon reproductions that inspired him to attempt similar compositions. He has retained both the book and an interest in the old master's work to the present day.

Fuertes, an American painter, strove to capture the individual characteristics or "personality" of his subjects. Like Audubon, he placed them in the proper setting, but by including two or more examples of each species in a single painting, he was able to reveal a great deal about how birds interact with their surroundings and each other. In another departure from previous convention, Fuertes did not place subjects at the centre of his composition, with meagre foliage to back them up. Instead, he favored highly developed visual elements, designed to draw a viewer's eye *into* the picture. His paintings convey a compelling intimacy which makes us feel that we are immersed in the landscape, not peering at it from a distance. By integrating accurate bird studies with such carefully crafted background scenes, Fuertes did more to raise nature painting to the level of fine art than any of his predecessors, and Loates considers him "a greater technician" than Audubon.

Loates' third mentor, Archibald Thorburn, was a British artist who first introduced "mood" to wildlife portrayals. Thorburn executed many of his paintings on sheets of tinted paper, so as to evoke a certain tone or atmosphere. For example, a robin might be presented on grey paper to suggest an overcast sky or afternoon rain. Often Thorburn would strengthen his compositions with a watercolor "wash"—a style that Loates would later adapt to bird paintings such as *Golden Eagle* and *The Bald Eagle*.

Extraordinarily enough, the legacy of Audubon, Fuertes and Thorburn is evident in Glen Loates' earliest "paintings," done when he was six years old. His prized collection of animal picture books and nature magazine clippings—hoarded the way that most little boys collect bubblegum cards—contained examples of their work. So, in what must have struck his parents as a startlingly precocious response, Glen embarked on his first crude attempts to copy what he'd seen, using crayons and colored pencils.

Almost from infancy, the world of nature had captured Glen's imagination. During those first six years, he and his twin brother Bernard lived with their parents and two older brothers in a flat on Toronto's Mount Pleasant Road, quite near the city centre. Despite the neighborhood's urban atmosphere, it was in many ways an ideal place for a budding naturalist, since the family's apartment was situated just north of the sprawling Mount Pleasant Cemetery. Its wooded areas offered Glen numerous opportunities to observe a wide variety of birds and small mammals first-hand—the cardinals, bluejays, Baltimore orioles and scarlet tanagers, the groundhogs, rabbits, chipmunks and squirrels.

Glen's interest in art also stemmed directly from his home environment. His father, Albert Loates, was a talented amateur painter and commercial designer, and Glen was fond of watching him at work in the enclosed back porch that served as a simple studio. Although Mr. Loates never gave Glen actual lessons, the boy picked up any number of useful tips, some of which he continues to make use of today. For example, his father would often begin by "roughing in" a design with bold smears of chalk to compose and balance the elements of an advertising layout. Glen employs a similar technique, making several preliminary sketches with watercolor washes to get a feel for a painting's overall design.

It was in his father's studio that Glen made his first attempts to draw what he'd actually *seen* in nature. "There was a light on the back porch that used to attract moths," he recalls. "I was fascinated by the delicate structure of their wings, so I captured some specimens and tried to sketch the intricate patterns using pencils and crayons. As an exercise, it was the best thing I could have done, but I grew terribly frustrated." Not surprisingly, given the tools at hand, these ventures were conspicuously unsuccessful, but Glen persevered, redrawing each subject over and over again until it looked "right" to him. Glen's mother saved many of his drawings from this period, and they survive today—evidence of the acute observations of a highly gifted pre-schooler.

When Glen was seven,
his family moved to Willowdale, today a
bustling Toronto suburb, but at that time an almost
rural haven. The fields, ravines, woods and streams
within easy walking distance of the house were perfect places
for a young naturalist to wander in search of exciting subjects,
and Glen began to take paper and pencils with him wherever he
chanced to roam.

Family outings during this period included frequent visits to
Toronto's Riverdale Zoo, where Glen first encountered more exotic
mammals and birds—the peacocks, flamingos, lions, tigers and apes.
He also found new inspiration at a local movie theater, where his
parents or Walter and Jim, his older brothers, would take him to see
Walt Disney nature films and cartoon features.

Today, Glen remembers with the utmost clarity his first viewing of Disney's classic *The Living Desert*: "I was overwhelmed by the
beauty of it all—the photography, the drama of animals filmed
in their natural habitat. It was a chunk of life,
thrown up on the screen. There were
battle scenes in which wasps and
tarantulas fought each other,
slow-motion sequences showing a
red-tail hawk swooping down and
attacking a rattlesnake, and footage
of bobcats and other predators going
about their business unaware of the
cameramen.

"I was thrilled by the life-and-death struggles and pursuits.

23

It opened my eyes to a totally new aspect of nature that I knew I'd someday try to capture on paper. It made me realize the importance of making first-hand observations in the wild, so as to portray the animals' movements and interrelationships realistically. I felt that through my own research I could capture in my drawing what Disney had achieved on film, but I had to go out and do a lot more field work."

Glen's opportunity came in 1954, when the Loates family moved closer to the Don River Valley, a favorite painting place for generations of Canadian artists. All that year, he spent his weekends hiking and exploring with his brother Bernard, sketching the valley's endless variety of insects, flowers, small mammals and birds.

Then, in 1955, an event occurred which was to alter the course of Glen's life. Fred Brigden, an accomplished watercolorist, illustrator and co-founder of one of Canada's largest commercial art houses, was invited to address the students at Glen's school. Brigden was in his mid-80s, but, to Glen, he seemed to have the vitality of a man 30 years younger: "He was white-haired, but marvelously dynamic. The way he spoke captured your whole being."

When Brigden finished speaking, Glen shyly approached and showed the artist several of his colored pencil drawings of butterflies and other insect life. Impressed with what he

saw, Brigden invited Glen to visit his studio, with a more complete selection. The following Saturday, Glen packed up a sampling of his animal drawings, sketches of Disney characters and original cartoons, hopped on his bicycle and peddled anxiously to the studio, located atop a hill overlooking the Don. After showing Glen examples of his own work and allowing him to tour the premises, Brigden examined the material, sorting it into two piles. One contained the cartoons; the other, Glen's sketches of birds, grasses, insects and animals.

"Forget these," Brigden said, pointing to the cartoons. "That's all been done before. *This* is what you should be concentrating on. These sketches show originality, because you painted them from life."

In the year that followed, Glen became a regular visitor to the studio, where the aging master instructed his protégé in watercolor technique. With quiet patience, he explained the intricacies of stretching watercolor paper to prevent it from buckling when damp, how to mix colors, how to work with transparent and opaque paints, and other basic skills. Under such expert guidance, Glen soon became at ease with the watercolor medium. Today, he remembers Brigden as the only true teacher he ever had. "He armed me with the technical knowledge I needed to progress from sketching in pen and crayon to making finished, full-color paintings. What's more, he gave me the encouragement and direction I needed to continue drawing and painting from nature. He could see a talent that I wasn't aware of, although he wasn't a wildlife artist. The tragedy is that he died very shortly after we'd met. He was gone before I could thank him, so the only way to show my thanks is by doing what I'm doing now."

Brigden's intervention came at a crucial point, when Glen was becoming more and more interested in cartoon animation, influenced of course by Disney. He remembers that he spent days making little "flip books," in which he'd draw the progression of an animal's movements on consecutive pages of a notepad. When quickly thumbed, these created a nice approximation of animated movement: "I wanted to get the feeling of how a bird flies, how a cat walks. I drew fish swimming around and a horse jumping over a fence." But, while the thought of eventually creating animated films excited him greatly, Brigden's influence won out, and Glen decided to concentrate on "real" painting. It was a decision he never regretted—even though, at the time, "there certainly wasn't a wildlife market. There was barely a wildlife field."

As Glen's painting technique became increasingly more sophisticated, he found himself returning home after school each day, preferring to work in his basement studio rather than take part in team sports or extracurricular activities. "I was a terrible batter," he recalls, "and for some reason a very good runner. When it was time for baseball, they'd put me in the outfield, but I did okay in track." Still, most of his time was spent in solitude and introspection, perfecting his artistic skills, carefully clipping photographs and illustrations of animal life for future reference.

Occasionally he would assist his father with commercial art assignments, and became adept at photographic retouching. For one such project, Albert Loates called upon Glen's special talents to produce a daffodil for the Canadian Cancer Society's fund-raising campaign. Glen rendered a suitable drawing, then fashioned a plasticine model that was used to cast a three-dimensional master mold. Bear in mind, the next time you contribute to the society's annual Daffodil Day, that what you receive is a plastic facsimile of a 12-year-old boy's highly durable design.

In 1960, Glen arrived at Willowdale's Northmount Junior High School, where his interest in wildlife art received yet another boost. His science teacher, Stewart Calvert, was a natural history enthusiast and keen environmentalist. Calvert encouraged Glen to add illustrations to his science essays, urged him to pursue art as a

career seriously, and suggested that he might investigate painting nature studies for the greeting card market.

By the time Glen turned 16, his almost obsessive devotion to painting began to cause difficulties at school. Although he excelled in art and science, his progress in other courses was less than satisfactory, largely because he had little interest in pursuing academic studies. Eventually, his creative gifts won out, and in 1961 he left formal schooling behind.

First he attempted to find a job, walking the streets with his portfolio, but received "the royal boot" from employers who cited his lack of practical experience. Next he visited the Ontario College of Art, where he'd hoped to enroll in an animal anatomy course. To his surprise, no such course existed. And while the college's president, Sydney Watson, was impressed by Glen's obvious ability, he rejected his application. First, Watson said, Glen's academic credits were insufficient. More important, the college had little to offer anyone so exclusively devoted to wildlife painting. In effect, there was nothing the college could teach Glen that he didn't already know.

Temporarily stymied, Glen enrolled in a commercial art course offered by a Toronto private school. Although he had absolutely no interest in a career as "a designer of chocolate boxes and disposable coffee cups," he thought that a diploma—any old diploma—would gain entry to an art studio where he could find an outlet for his talents.

Thanks to Brigden's invaluable training and the practical experience gained while assisting with his father's assignments, Glen quickly mastered the basics of lettering, layout and design. Bored with such rudiments, he decided to drop out and search for work. When he announced his intentions to

Yellow-Shafted Flicker
May 14/67

27

bright red

white

red

winter breeded effect
black & white

white
patches

Yellow Bellied Sapsucker
April 16/67
Bayview at Sheppard Av.

the school's director, he was handed a diploma ("a fancy one, with a big gold sticker"), wished good luck, and sent on his way.

Armed with his wildlife portfolio and samples of the advertising layouts he'd created at the art school, Glen once again trudged to and fro between Toronto's advertising agencies and art houses. Eventually he found a job at the Dickenson Commercial Art Studios for a lowly $25 per week ("It was like a cleaning service—all the dirty work"). He retouched photographs for catalogues and product labels, swept the studio, washed paint pots and brushes, and ran errands when business was slow—hardly an auspicious beginning for a man whose work would presently be known to more people than that of any other living Canadian artist.

Nonetheless, his year's apprenticeship enabled Glen to meet a number of patrons who were to advance his career dramatically. His employer, Marjorie Dickenson, introduced him to Charles Mathews, of the Sampson and Mathews printing firm, who hired Glen to paint a dozen Canadian wildflower studies for a 1964 Toronto Dominion Bank calendar. Glen was elated to receive his first commission, and quickly produced color renderings of trilliums, wild columbines, jack-in-the-pulpits and other native plant life. Although the assignment demanded anonymity, with the result that he was not allowed to sign the paintings, Glen's talents were finally and formally acknowledged.

Later that same year, Glen was asked by the R.G. McLean printing firm for six more wildflower paintings, which were reproduced in quantity and sold by mail. In addition to a handsome $1600 fee for his first freelance assignment, Glen was at last permitted to sign his work.

While Glen was still at Dickenson, Stewart Calvert, his former teacher, brought him to the attention of Ottelyn Addison, a frequent contributor to the *Ontario Naturalist Magazine.* Mrs. Addison invited Glen to illustrate her articles, and over an eight-month period he produced numerous pen and ink sketches of wildflowers, plantlife, birds and fish. Each tiny drawing meant only a few dollars in hand, but the contacts that resulted were

to have immediate effect.

Mrs. Addison's son, Bill, himself a naturalist, introduced Glen to Jim Baillie, an ornithologist at the Royal Ontario Museum and a well-known writer on bird life. Baillie in turn introduced him to his colleagues, among them, Terence Shortt, the ROM's chief artist and one of Canada's most outstanding bird painters. In addition to giving Glen the benefit of their vast experience, Baillie and Shortt offered him access to the museum's collection of bird and mammal skins, a resource he continues to use today.

Terry Shortt quickly became an admirer of Glen's work, and in 1965 organized his first one-man show, which appeared in the museum's rotunda for several weeks. This exhibition of 50 watercolors and drawings was viewed by a large audience of wildlife art collectors, many of whom remained committed patrons. It also provided much-needed international exposure when, the following year, it moved to the Museum of Natural History in Buffalo, New York.

Meanwhile, Glen's illustrations in the *Ontario Naturalist* had led to a commission from the Federation of Ontario

Naturalists to paint a wildlife study for its 1964 Christmas card. He was paid only $150 for a miniature watercolor of two cardinals perched on a pine bough—but, as he soon discovered, the effect this assignment would have on his career far exceeded its initial monetary value.

One of the cards found its way to Gene Aliman, art director of *The Canadian*, a magazine distributed with the weekend editions of newspapers coast to coast. He immediately recognized the wide appeal of Glen's work, and was keen to include a series of similar bird portraits in his 1965 Christmas issue. Accordingly, he commissioned Glen to submit eight songbird paintings for the magazine's consideration.

Glen spent the next six months on this single assignment. He chose to employ the "photographic" style of his earlier calendar illustrations, with each main subject isolated and sharply defined against a blurred, "out of focus" background. Of the eight works submitted, four were chosen for reproduction: the Steller's jays, eastern bluebirds, Baltimore orioles and Bohemian waxwings. In the weeks following their appearance, *The Canadian* received an unprecedented amount of mail—literally sacks of letters proclaiming the discovery of a major new talent.

Many of the letters were from children, and for the first time Glen realized that his work held special appeal for young nature lovers. Many described how they used his pictures for school projects, pasted them in scrapbooks or hung them on bedroom walls. Some simply encouraged him to keep painting, and said they looked forward to seeing more of his animal art in future issues of the

Blueberry Hill
A Gomas

Sap
Green colour

White
waxy appearance

May Apple Podophyllum peltatum
Col May 27/69 Drawn from life
Brimley rd. near French Ave.
Toronto Ont.

Raw Umber

magazine. Reading this enormous outpouring of fan mail reminded Glen of his boyhood attraction to Walt Disney's animals, and he was thrilled to think that his work had struck a similar chord.

Glen received $1000 for the songbird commission, then sold the original paintings for $700 each. The money he received for six months' work scarcely represented instant riches, but the immense popularity of this first series resulted in many more assignments from *The Canadian*. Two were completed the following year: *Game Fish*, which included rainbow trout, muskellunge, small-mouth bass and walleye; and *Game Birds*, featuring a ruffed grouse, a band-tailed pigeon, a pair of Canada geese, mallard ducks, a ring-necked pheasant and an American woodcock. Both projects necessitated a great deal of research at the museum and in the field. Since fish lose their color quickly when removed from water, Glen netted live specimens, which he painted while they swam about in a portable aquarium. He went snorkelling in remote Ontario lakes to study proper environmental settings, and confirmed the accuracy of his observations by showing his sketches and preliminary studies to

experts at the Royal Ontario Museum.

The following year, *The Canadian* gave Glen his most challenging assignment to date: a pictorial feature depicting Canada's big game animals. Chosen subjects were a moose, a cougar, a pair of white-tailed deer, a mountain goat, a black bear and a grizzly bear. To observe these animals in their natural habitat meant that Glen had to make his first extended journeys into the wilderness. He'd always been fond of camping out, and remembers that, as a boy, he'd often bicycled to the eastern outskirts of Toronto, near the site of today's Metro Zoo, where he'd pitch a tent and remain for days, "sketching anything that moved." As an adult, he'd been as far afield as Ontario's Manitoulin Island in search of data for his bird portraits. But these lengthier trips, undertaken during the summer of 1967, were another matter entirely. The first brought Glen and Bernard to the northern Quebec town of Chibougamau, then by small float plane and canoe to that province's unpopulated interior.

Having survived a rough passage through turbulent rapids, ("hanging on for dear life") and an even narrower escape from an adjacent whirlpool ("taking on water and spinning like a top"), the two canoeists were confronted with a remarkable sight: "There, standing in the water, almost close enough to reach out and touch, was an enormous moose. His body was completely submerged except for the hump of his back. Startled by our arrival, he raised

his head and scooped up a huge clump of waterlilies with his antlers. Despite his clumsy appearance, he quickly sprang ashore, trailing the lilies like a veil and glaring at us over his shoulder. I was still shaken up by the whirlpool, but I grabbed my pencils and started sketching furiously as he slipped into the forest."

Glen's finished portrait of the startled moose appeared on the cover of the February 3rd, 1968 issue of *The Canadian*—without the dangling lily pads, since Glen feared that their comical aspect would detract from the otherwise powerful image of the bulky creature, splashing and angered, fixing the interlopers with its baleful gaze.

Upon his return from Quebec, Glen found it necessary to visit western Canada, to obtain his first field experience of mountain goats and bears. Accompanied by Bernard and their friend Don Gray, a film producer who wished to make a documentary of Glen's working methods, he set out for the Yukon. The story of this ill-fated adventure has been told in *The Art of Glen Loates*, and it stands as a classic illustration of the theory that anything that *can* go wrong, will. A local guide who promised to lead Glen and his companions to herds of wild game ("From our first meeting, I had serious reservations about his ability to lead us *anywhere*") loaded them into an ancient former lifeboat ("It reminded me a lot of the scow that Humphrey Bogart piloted in *The African Queen*"). The guide proceeded to tow the unfortunate trio up a particularly nasty

mountain, where he shot a goat out of season, turned the gun on his frightened clients, and finally abandoned them to their fate.

After a perilous descent, including an almost-fatal mishap while crossing a glacier and a night spent clinging to the inhospitable rock face, Glen and his party returned to Vancouver, having produced few sketches and virtually no film footage.

After spending a few days recuperating from their experiences, Glen and Don headed north again, to the tiny Pacific coast town of Rivers Inlet, B.C. Here Don was able to film Glen at work in the surrounding countryside, and much of this footage was used in his award-winning documentary *Color it Living*. This portion of the trip, at least, proved to be an important visual experience. Glen's sketches of bald eagles would be retrieved from his files 14 years later, when he began work on his life-size portrait, *The Bald Eagle*. He managed to catch a glimpse of several grizzlies which, along with the mountain goat studies, enabled him to complete his assignment. Also, the B.C. interior's rugged terrain made a lasting and favorable impression, with the result that Glen has returned to the region on numerous occasions.

The publication of Glen's *Big Game* paintings in *The Canadian* spurred another flood of mail and with the exception of the moose portrait, which he decided to keep, the originals were quickly sold.

These paintings are highly significant, because they signalled a marked shift in Glen's style. Three of the subjects are captured in dramatic poses: the moose in irate retreat, the cougar and grizzly bear in attacking postures. Unlike many of his earlier portraits, background detail is kept to a bare minimum, to avoid distracting the observer from the subject's power. This was a departure that offered the first evidence of Glen's increasing fascination with Oriental compositions. He had decided to abandon the blurred backgrounds of his early "photographic" style in favor of a new direction.

"The last thing I was trying to do was to *mimic* the effects created by the camera," he says. "But that's how many people interpreted my early approach. The camera freezes a moment in time, but it's limited and non-discriminating. I can go further, because I've got the freedom to add or remove detail, to create a prevailing atmosphere. With the *Big Game* series, I reduced the background of each painting to light

Steller's Jay

Timber Wolf

tail

black tip

pads

left foreleg

Cortes—79

tints of watercolor wash, then concentrated on building the weight and balance of the compositions around the animal's pose, and foreground details such as trees, logs and rocks. I was collecting books on Oriental art at that time, and I was strongly influenced by the landscape, animal and flower studies created by many Chinese and Japanese artists. They're absolutely flawless. Nothing is included unless it's totally significant; every item really *means* something. I decided to adapt to my own work that sort of approach to composition, that use of white space, and weight and color balance."

Technically, the *Big Game* portraits reveal Glen's mastery of a dry brush technique with which he'd been experimenting for several years. By applying paint, India ink and Chinese white drawing ink with a specially pointed brush, Glen devised a method of accurately depicting the textures and partings of an animal's fur, the tension in the muscles beneath. Few other wildlife painters, whatever their medium, have achieved the rich tone and realistic sense evidenced by these half-dozen watercolors. Variations on this demanding style would later appear in such major works as *Timber Wolves*, *Canada Lynx*, and *White-tailed Deer*.

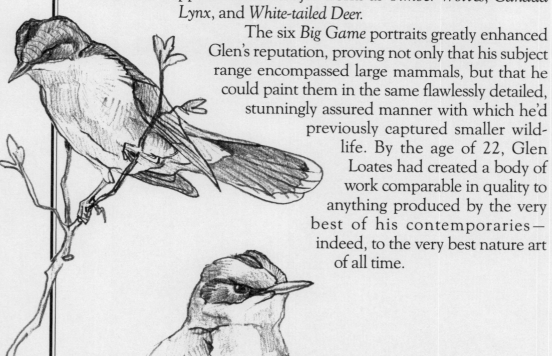

The six *Big Game* portraits greatly enhanced Glen's reputation, proving not only that his subject range encompassed large mammals, but that he could paint them in the same flawlessly detailed, stunningly assured manner with which he'd previously captured smaller wildlife. By the age of 22, Glen Loates had created a body of work comparable in quality to anything produced by the very best of his contemporaries— indeed, to the very best nature art of all time.

A TURNING POINT

THE YEAR 1970 MARKED A VITAL TURNING POINT IN BOTH GLEN'S PROFESSIONAL CAREER AND HIS PERSONAL LIFE. WHILE WORKING IN A SMALL STUDIO at his brother Bernard's newly established publishing firm, Glen met Sally Harding, a schoolteacher who was spending the summer doing layout and pasteup work. Soon they were dating regularly, and would marry in June the following year.

Most of Glen's creative energies during 1970 were spent preparing a series of wildflower and mammal paintings for *The Canadian*. The *Canadian Wildflowers* collection was published in the magazine's May 16th issue, and included striking portraits of morning glories, swamp irises, evening primroses, day lilies, purple-flowering raspberries, and the turk's-cap lily. Glen's crisp, delicate treatments seem reminiscent of the nineteenth century English watercolorists—simple, direct presentations utilizing a minimum of background detail. This same style would reappear in many of his later bird portraits, such as *Blue Jays* and *Eastern Cardinals*. To render the subtle color shadings correctly, Glen first painted numerous studies of the flowers in their natural settings, then transported them to his studio to serve as models for the finished works.

By 1970, Glen's art had become widely known throughout North America. In September of that year, 41 of his works were shown at the Jesse Besser Museum of Natural History at Alpena, Michigan. It was Glen's first major American show since the Buffalo Museum exhibit of 1966, and the publicity he received resulted in several additional exhibitions and numerous commissions from private collectors, as well as welcome attention in the pages of *Audubon* magazine. Its editors would shortly publish a lengthy profile, along with several reproductions of Glen's paintings. Later, thanks to a warm response from *Audubon*'s readership, Glen's work was featured with some regularity in the publication's "Gallery of Wildlife Art" section.

In 1971, *The Canadian* featured Glen's *Animals of Field and Forest* series, including portraits of a raccoon, a red fox, an eastern

This world is but canvas to our imaginations.
Henry David Thoreau

flying squirrel, a skunk, and a meadow vole. In these works, Glen continued his investigation of encounters between antagonistic species, a theme that would later become almost a trademark. The red fox, for example, pursues a pheasant, while the skunk is about to pounce on a bronze click beetle.

During the summer of 1971, Glen Loates became the first wildlife painter to be given a one-man exhibition at the McMichael Gallery in Kleinburg, Ontario. The McMichael Collection includes the country's largest selection of paintings by the Group of Seven, along with the work of Inuit and Indian artists. Several exhibition areas are set aside for showings by prominent contemporary artists, and two such rooms were devoted to Glen's watercolors. He was deeply honored to see his paintings housed with landscapes by such eminent figures as A.Y. Jackson, Lawren Harris, and Tom Thompson.

By this time, Glen's work was in such demand that he found himself unable to meet the many requests from gallery owners wishing to exhibit his art and from collectors offering him handsome commissions to paint specific subjects. He had even less time for, and virtually no interest in, developing his broader commercial potential. On a relatively small scale, *The Canadian* had printed and distributed reproductions of paintings that appeared in the magazine, and the overwhelming response to this program suggested to Glen that there existed a much larger and virtually untapped market for inexpensive reproductions of his work.

Glen began by talking to a number of agents and artists' representatives, but found that "things just didn't seem to work out." Fortunately, the best solution emerged close to home. Bernard's publishing firm offered both the interest and the skills required to undertake the task. In fact,

Glen began to rely on Bernard for all sorts of assistance with his business dealings, and within a short time they had established an artist-manager relationship that flourished for over ten years. During that period Glen, with Bernard's assistance and encouragement, was able to devote himself entirely to painting wildlife art while Bernard handled all his business affairs.

In 1972, Bernard Loates established Nature Impressions Limited, which began to print and market affordable reproductions in all sizes and formats, including greeting cards. The company reproduced over 150 of Glen's works, and tens of thousands of copies of his most popular paintings have been sold throughout Canada, the United States and Europe.

The great success of these ventures prompted Bernard to explore the possibility of publishing a collection of Glen's art in book form. But no ordinary book would suffice. Bernard had admired the quality art books and portfolios of limited edition prints which, until then, had been produced almost exclusively in the United States and abroad. In 1974, he began work on a volume which he felt could be made available the following year, in two distinct formats: a limited edition, and a smaller, less expensive "trade" edition for mass distribution.

In the event, his timetable was hopelessly optimistic. After

numerous color printing firms had turned him down, claiming the quality he demanded for the deluxe edition was impossible to attain, Bernard spend almost four years solving the technical problems on his own. He brought a color etcher from Europe, purchased a special printing press, and devised a unique method of making ink remain on the surface of porous, all-rag paper stock. The paper itself had to be custom-made, as did the book's linen slipcase and outer display box.

Finally, after a thousand disappointments and delays, *The Art of Glen Loates* was published in 1977, in a limited edition of 300 copies. The book set new standards of excellence in Canadian publishing, and garnered instant acclaim. Each volume was handbound in Brazilian steerhide and encased in a cherrywood box; each page was edged with 24-carat gold leaf; and a signed and numbered lithograph depicting a North American bison was included with each copy. At its initial pre-publication price of $600 (a price established in 1975), the limited edition quickly sold out. Five years later, copies were being resold for as much as $6000 each. And over that same period, almost 50 000 copies of the trade edition found their way into the hands of an appreciative public, making it one of the best-selling volumes of any living Canadian artist's work.

Prior to the book's publication, Glen had received further recognition in both Canada and the United States. In 1974, he was elected to full membership of the Royal Canadian Academy, becoming the first wildlife painter to be invited to join this prestigious association. And in March of that year, he was approached by Cornell University's Department of Ornithology, at Sapsucker Woods, New York. Many of the world's leading wildlife artists have exhibited at this internationally renowned institution, including Louis Agassiz Fuertes, Sir Peter Scott and Roger Tory Peterson. Glen was asked to mount a show of more than 40 watercolors depicting both birds and mammals. To his delight, he received both personal praise and extremely complimentary reviews in the university's highly critical newsletter.

By the mid-1970s, wildlife art was enjoying a phenomenal growth in popular interest, due to both the previous decade's ecology

Belted Kingfisher
Echo Lake
April 23/67

movement and a general trend towards representational art of every kind. In 1975, the Royal Ontario Museum held a major exhibition entitled *Animals in Art*, bringing together the best of contemporary wildlife painting from around the world, along with masterpieces from the past. Glen's contribution was *Red Fox and Ring-Necked Pheasant*, a major watercolor completed that year. Seeing it hung beside his childhood heroes, Audubon, Fuertes and Thorburn—especially since this was his first opportunity to view the originals of paintings he'd admired in reproduction so long ago—convinced Glen Loates that he'd truly arrived at last.

The late 1970s and early 1980s have been among Glen's most productive years. During this period, he perfected the style and technique for which he's famous today, moving from his early "photographic" approach to portrait studies in which both background and foreground are often highly developed, adding depth to a depiction of the subject's total environment.

The paintings executed since 1977 reveal not only Glen's phenomenal draftsmanship and exquisite brushwork, but also his remarkable ability to capture the essence of his subjects in a single, characteristic pose. In addition, these recent works explore Glen's continuing fascination with two themes: dramatic confrontations between enemy species, and powerful, direct portrayals of predatory birds and mammals in striking postures.

The painting *Golden Eagle* offers an example of the first category: the subject has already conquered its victim, and we witness the predator about to savor its spoils.

On the other hand, the paintings *Timber Wolves* and *The Bald Eagle* offer an *implied* domination over another species. These two works suggest ferocity and aggression without actually depicting the subjects in battle or pursuit. Instead, they depict what photographer Henri Cartier-Bresson termed "the decisive moment"—the instant in which a subject's most significant aspect reveals itself to the viewer.

For his bald eagle painting, Glen chose to capture the moment in which only one talon has established a foothold on the pine stump, before the bird has balanced itself and lowered its wings—indirectly, though unmistakably, stating its powerful striking force. With *Timber Wolves*, he invites us to actually participate in nature's drama. The wolves look up with chilling stares; *we* become the prey they've been stalking along the snowy hillock. The sense of anticipated action is heightened by the wolves' expressions; we expect them to bare their teeth and pounce out from the page. For added impact, Glen painted the wolves almost life-size, on a sheet of linen measuring 142 cm by 106 cm (56 inches by 42 inches).

These paintings also reveal a fundamental shift in Glen's approach to composition. In the past, he'd often painted his animals in compositions that "floated" in a large area of white space. But since the late 1970s, the subjects tend to fill an entire sheet. This simple yet remarkably effective device adds extreme impact, suggesting a force and tension *within* the animal portrayed. We feel the weight and immediacy of these subjects; in Glen's words, "It's as if you've just drawn back the curtains, and there they are."

Another unifying factor in Glen's more recent paintings is a painstaking attention to the details of a subject's natural habitat. The bald eagle, for example, is shown landing on a beautifully rendered lodge-pole pine stump, typical of the Pacific beaches where eagles tend to congregate. The golden eagle perches on a slab of granite veined with rose quartz, a rock formation found in the Algoma region of northern Ontario where Glen made his preliminary sketches. To ensure such details are as life-like as his primary subjects, Glen gathers samples of rocks, grasses and other vegetation while on his field trips, taking them home with him for subsequent examination.

Glen's output during the period between 1978 and 1982 is even more remarkable when one considers the fact that he was in physical pain for much of the time, as the result of an accident he suffered in July 1978. He recalls the mishap somewhat philosophically today, noting the supreme irony that a trained naturalist who'd spent much of his life pursuing animals in the wild should come to grief while chasing his pet kitten.

"It happened just after a rainstorm," he remembers. "The kitten was playing out behind our house, when a neighbor's German shepherd came into the garden. The kitten darted off towards a rocky embankment, and I ran quickly along the hilltop, trying to get to her before the dog did. As I reached down to scoop her up, I slipped on the grass and went skidding down the embankment, coming to a stop against a rock. I felt an excruciating pain in my left hip; for several minutes I couldn't move at all, but I eventually managed to get up and hobble back to the house with the kitten under my arm."

The weeks that followed were spent in worsening pain and Glen was confined to his bed for most of the summer. At first, his doctor was unable to diagnose the problem, and simply recommended that he stay off his feet while further tests were made. Although unable to move without shooting pains in his leg, Glen managed to complete a major painting that fall, working flat on his back with the aid of an adjustable easel his brother-in-law arranged above his bed. This portrait, a study of two harlequin ducks, was slated for inclusion in a retrospective of

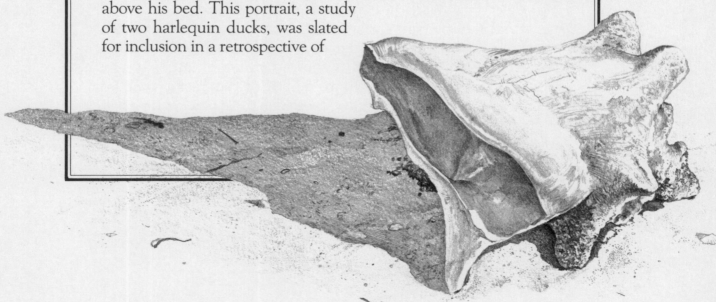

Goldeneye's

his work to be held in October at the Vancouver Aquarium in Stanley Park. Limited edition reproductions were to be sold at the exhibition to raise funds for the aquarium's research projects, and Glen was determined not to disappoint this worthy cause. Somehow he managed to complete the task on time. Then, against his doctor's orders, he flew to Vancouver for the opening ceremonies, which he attended with the aid of crutches and a wheelchair.

Shortly after his return home, Glen was admitted to hospital for exploratory surgery on his hip and a corrective operation to relieve the pain he suffered whenever he moved his leg. Confined to a hospital bed for nine weeks, and stricken with boredom and frustration, he kept a two-volume journal, illustrated with pen-and-ink cartoons that poke gentle fun at hospital life. These humorous yet poignant drawings suggest the more relaxed and whimsical style Glen might have developed had he pursued his other boyhood ambition. Certainly they proved popular with the doctors and nursing staff, and were shown, by means of an overhead projector, to a visiting delegation of hospital administrators who'd come to attend a medical conference.

Gradually, between bouts of gruelling physiotherapy and a lingering convalescence at home, Glen returned to work in the spring of 1979 on a project begun before his accident—a limited edition portfolio of 25 original lithographs depicting the winter birds of North America. Entitled *A Coming of Winter*, it had originally been conceived as a collection of high quality color reproductions of Glen's watercolor paintings. Its subjects included cardinals, blue jays, gray jays, great horned owls, marsh hawks, ravens and other non-migrating species. But after creating several preliminary drawings, Glen decided to produce each image as an original sepia-tinted print.

"I wanted to create something different," he says, "something that would be considered a work of art, not just an elaborate field guide. After much experimenting, I chose to tint the images with a series of brown and yellow inks, giving each print the appearance of an

Great Horned Owl

GOATES

Soft Ruff

Long whiskers around bill

mouse

After J.E. Patterson Photo
Bear Creek May 1928

Kennicotti eats almost any animal food.
It catches night-flying beetles and moths
and takes birds, small mammals, and
even earthworms. Its diet depends
largely upon what is most readily
obtained.

· This large, dark-colored screech owl is found
in the humid, northwest-coast region.

COATES —1973—

Screech Owl
Otus asio Kennicotti

old master's etching. This made sense from an ornithological stand-point as well, since many of the birds are in fact gray or brown-shaded, while most of the others lose much of their color in winter."

Creating this effect required a great deal more time and effort than painting a series of color portraits for reproduction. Glen began by drawing comprehensive pencil sketches of each bird, which were transferred onto metal lithographic plates using a revolutionary process devised by his brother Bernard. Up to seven ink colors were combined to achieve the soft, rich tonal values he desired. And, to further complicate the procedure, a separate plate had to be made for each color.

Due to the complexities of the printing process and the great detail necessary to portray each bird, this one project took over two years to complete. But the end result more than justified Glen's approach, and many collectors acknowledge the folio as one of his most important accomplishments. All 125 copies of *A Coming of Winter* were sold at a pre-publication price of $2500 each; but by the time they were released in 1981, investors and art dealers were reselling them for more than double that amount.

Also in 1979, Glen embarked on a series of four sculptures portraying endangered mammals, a commission he'd received the previous year from the Audubon Society to commemorate its upcoming 75th anniversary. Each four-figure set was to be cast in pewter, and sold for $1200 as part of the society's fund-raising campaign.

Few people realize that Glen is a gifted sculptor, and could, if he chose, produce excellent finished work. Most of his efforts, however, serve only as preliminary aids in the completion of his paintings. He continues to work in plasticine, his boyhood medium: "It's infinitely pliable, and never dries out. Used over a wire frame, it enables me to think in three dimensions. It's a very challenging exercise, and I look forward to doing more sculpture in the future; but, for the moment, it's usually just another tool."

The Audubon commission, however, demanded that Glen follow through to the end product. The society was so eager to have him do so that they developed a new process for making molds from plasticine, rather than the more usual clay. They insisted on

picking the four animals to be portrayed: a Florida panther, a key deer, a silver-tipped grizzly and a timber wolf. Each was caught in a dramatic pose: the bear tearing apart a rotted lodge-pole pine stump in search of insects; the deer poised ready to leap over a log; the wolf standing on a snowy embankment with tilted head, as if howling at the moon in some lonely northern forest. Glen's original design for the panther, hungrily pursuing a rabbit, was vetoed by society officials who thought it might offend tender-hearted purchasers. Glen obligingly removed the quarry, redesigning the piece with the panther bounding gracefully from beneath a bush.

In recent years, Glen's hip injury has prevented him from making extended journeys into the wilderness. Nevertheless, during the summer of 1981 he travelled by train to Moosonee, Ontario, where he chartered an airplane and flew up the James Bay coast to the boreal forest. There, on the edge of the tundra, he made pencil and watercolor sketches of numerous arctic birds, from which three paintings evolved. One, a detailed study entitled *Lesser Scaup Ducks*, was actually completed on location.

The James Bay excursion was Glen's first field trip following his operation. He returned home ready to resume painting with renewed vigor, and within two months he'd completed a major commission begun earlier that year, a bird portrait entitled *Golden Eagle*.

Predatory birds are some of Glen's favorite subjects. "If you look at a cardinal or a bluejay," he says, "it has a certain charm, a subtle beauty. But the actions of an eagle or a hawk about to swoop down on its prey, or spreading its wings to cover its victim after a kill, have a dynamic appeal I find absolutely fascinating. The predators are almost spellbinding. They demand your attention; they *expect* it of you."

With the golden eagle painting, Glen deliberately set himself a problem in draftsmanship, by depicting the bird life-size, with its wings outspread in a "mantling" attitude—a pose that required him to include the most minute details of virtually all its wing feathers. His task was further complicated by the need to foreshorten the eagle's wingspan, in order to give the work an illusion of depth and a three-dimensional effect. He overcame these difficulties by using a variety of reference materials, including sketches he'd made of golden eagles in northern Ontario's Algoma Canyon, an eagle "skin" from the Royal Ontario Museum, an outstretched wing and tail obtained from a taxidermist, and numerous photographs of the birds in characteristic poses.

Measuring 127 cm by 152 cm (50 inches by 60 inches), *Golden Eagle* was the largest and most technically complex bird portrait Glen had attempted. Artistically, the painting is a triumph of watercolor technique. Glen's phenomenal skill is evidenced not only by his uncannily realistic treatment of the bird itself, but also in the detail lavished on subsidiary elements—the dead rabbit's fur, the rocks and grasses in the foreground.

But *Golden Eagle* heralded an even more ambitious undertaking. To commemorate the 200th anniversary of the bald eagle's designation as America's official symbol, President Ronald Reagan declared 1982 "The Year of the Eagle." Glen was prompted to mark the event by attempting a life-size portrait of the bird of prey. He began by reviewing the sketches he'd completed in 1968 near Rivers Inlet, B.C. From these, he selected one which struck him as most representative of the eagle's facial expression, and painted a detailed study of the bird's head. Satisfied with this portrait, he then proceeded to make several rough sketches of the body, set in various

American Goldfinch

positions and observed from different angles. He finally chose an arresting pose with the eagle's wings outspread as it lands on a stump.

Glen recalls that the highly charged symbolism of this particular subject imposed a number of difficulties in presentation: "Because the bald eagle is a national symbol, I had to ensure that the bird's demeanor couldn't be misconstrued. If I'd portrayed it in an aggressive posture—perhaps attacking another animal—it could have been interpreted as a glorification of America's military might. On the other hand, if I'd followed through with my original concept, and painted a rear view of the bird with its wings lowered and head in profile, some people would have imagined a negative connotation—America turning its back on the world."

These considerations were of supreme importance, because Glen intended to approach the Canadian government with a bold suggestion. He wanted the painting to be an official gift to the American people, and hoped that the publicity generated by its presentation would serve to increase public awareness of the bald eagle's plight as an endangered species.

The entire project took Glen seven months to complete. Apart from his concerns regarding the most appropriate pose, he was faced with the arduous task of sketching and painting in precise details of the wing and body feathers—a staggering prospect, considering that the pose he'd selected required him to paint the eagle's two-metre wingspan life-size.

Quite simply, *The Bald Eagle* is a masterpiece, and Glen rightly considers it the best bird of prey painting he's done. It captures both the regal quality of the bird in flight and its most graceful posture as it gently returns to earth—a sense of movement greatly heightened by Glen's attention to infinitesimal detail. From a distance the eagle's feather pattern appears to be a rough mosaic of odd shapes and textures, but close examination reveals the superb technique meticulously brought to bear on every visible portion of the bird's anatomy.

Yet, despite this painstaking attention to surface exactitude, the painting's real greatness lies in Glen's ability to penetrate mere outer realism, drawing us into the very essence of the bird. Viewing the original, you can imagine how the downy softness of the eagle's nape feathers would feel to the touch; marvel at the power of its wings suggested by a tension in the muscles across its shoulder plane and in the outward thrust of the primary feathers; sense the awesome ferocity laid bare by its facial expression. Shuddering with life, *The Bald Eagle* virtually screams for release from the two-dimensional confines of the watercolor paper.

In the fall of 1982, as the work neared completion and the Year of the Eagle drew to its close, Glen decided to approach Prime Minister Trudeau and obtain the Canadian government's endorsement of his gift. Glen's older brother Walter, a personal friend of Trudeau's, arranged a luncheon meeting. Trudeau responded positively, offering to accompany Glen to Washington and take part in the presentation. Hurried preparations were made through the Prime Minister's Office and American Embassy officials in Ottawa, and a date was set for Glen's reception at the White House.

On December 22nd, 1982, Glen Loates flew to Washington, carrying with him the eagle painting; the ceremony was slated for the following day. A conflict in Prime Minister Trudeau's schedule prevented him from attending, so Glen was accompanied by Canadian Ambassador Allan Gotlieb. In the Oval Office, surrounded by reporters, photographers and the blinding lights of television cameras, Glen was introduced to President Reagan. The two shook hands in front of the painting, and Glen gave a short speech. Reagan

thanked him profusely, complimenting him on what he termed "a breathtaking representation of America's symbol." Then, turning to the onlookers, Reagan added: "This beautiful piece of artwork will serve as a special reminder of the warm friendship and goodwill shared by our peoples."

Glen Loates is the first Canadian artist to present a painting personally to an American president. He was deeply touched by his reception, and his pleasure was increased upon learning that the portrait has been displayed where thousands of Americans may enjoy it. When not in the White House, *The Bald Eagle* is on public view at Washington's prestigious Smithsonian Institution.

These honors seem a more than fitting tribute. *The Bald Eagle* represents the crowning achievement to date of Glen's lifelong efforts to recreate the beauty of the wild, to convey the enduring sympathy he feels in the presence of nature's creatures. In a single work, he included virtually all the aspects of nature he finds so fascinating: beauty, action, drama, and the dominion of one species over others. At the same time, by choosing to paint this tragically endangered bird in such an affecting pose, he reminds us that his subject's survival rests precariously in our hands.

The Bald Eagle, like all his work, affirms that Glen's talents as artist and naturalist are bound inextricably together. And judging by his unrelenting commitment to his art and to the subjects he paints so lovingly, those talents will flourish and continue to grow for many years to come.

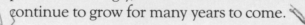

REFLECTION

GLEN LOATES IS A MAN IN LOVE WITH NATURE, TOTALLY AT EASE WITH THE ENVIRONMENT; HE REVELS IN EACH OPPORTUNITY TO BE OUT-OF-doors, accepting the ever-changing elements, becoming a part of what takes place around him. In the course of a typical year his field trips might take him to the more remote regions of Ontario, Quebec and British Columbia, far from the encroachments of civilization. His idea of a short weekend jaunt is a retreat to Algonquin Park, a vast wilderness area on the edge of the Canadian Shield he's come to know as a "second studio." Nothing excites him more than the prospect of nature untainted by man. "Even if I didn't paint, I'd still go," he says. "I simply love everything about it."

Every day, even while based at home, Glen attempts to spend at least some time outside the house. He may head for the woods at the bottom of his property, or pack a lunch and drive into the southern Ontario countryside in search of new subject matter or new background material for a work in progress.

To accompany Glen on these excursions is, literally, an eye-opening experience, a crash course in visual awareness. He can identify most birds from a great distance, by their calls or characteristic flight patterns. Each rustle in the undergrowth becomes a creature, long since cataloged in his mind; each wildflower blooms anew, illuminated by his wealth of anecdote and information. Every sense seems to be attuned as he strolls along, sketchpad and pencils in hand.

When a subject comes into view, Glen reacts with lightning speed, zoom-lens binoculars at the ready. He has an almost photographic memory. Years of training enable him to observe, absorb and record movements that last perhaps a fraction of a second. A rapidly executed sketch captures the essence of a bird or animal he may glimpse for only a moment. If the subject retreats, he continues to sketch, intuitively filling in details while they remain fresh in his mind's eye.

Most of Glen's concepts originate from first-hand observations

Come forth into the light of things
Let Nature be your teacher.
William Wordsworth

in the field. "No wildlife artist can be successful without obtaining an intimate understanding of the animals he paints, their movements and interactions. One of the greatest skills an artist can develop is the ability to retain a sufficient store of impressions that can be instantly recalled at need. A field trip isn't a waiting game; you have to know where to look and what to look for. You have to be aware of the signs that will lead you to an animal, and know by heart its nocturnal or daytime habits."

Although Glen is constantly thinking in terms of future paintings, most of his sketching trips are intended to augment a work already in progress. Every new portrait will find him on a quest for supportive images or fresh detail—the colors and textures of a forest setting, the precise manner in which sunlight filters through a woodland stream. Sometimes a field trip will inspire him to produce a landscape. Unlike his wildlife portraits, these paintings are relaxed and loose, almost abstract in the sense that many of Andrew Wyeth's works capture the essence of a scene by suggesting a mood or atmosphere, rather than concentrating on a single object. Indeed, Glen acknowledges a debt to Wyeth's influence. When painting preliminary studies, Glen will often capture sky, weather and lighting conditions in a series of small watercolors. These, along with the many treatments of his main subjects, will later be incorporated into finished works.

Glen now lives in Maple, Ontario, to the north of Toronto's constantly expanding city limits. His studio seems a model of disciplined order, with hardly a random smudge of paint in sight. Brushes, paints and pencils are neatly stacked on the steel and arborite draftsman's table that serves as an easel, illuminated by a stream of light from a pair of spotless windows.

The walls are decorated with examples of Glen's early work—mostly marine and plantlife studies—as well as somewhat blood-curdling reminders of nature red in tooth and claw: a dried and mounted bird-eating spider the size of a soup bowl competes for space with a drawing of a gruesome battle between a sperm whale and a giant squid. On the opposite wall, a teakwood display cabinet houses Glen's prized collection of Walt Disney memorabilia—

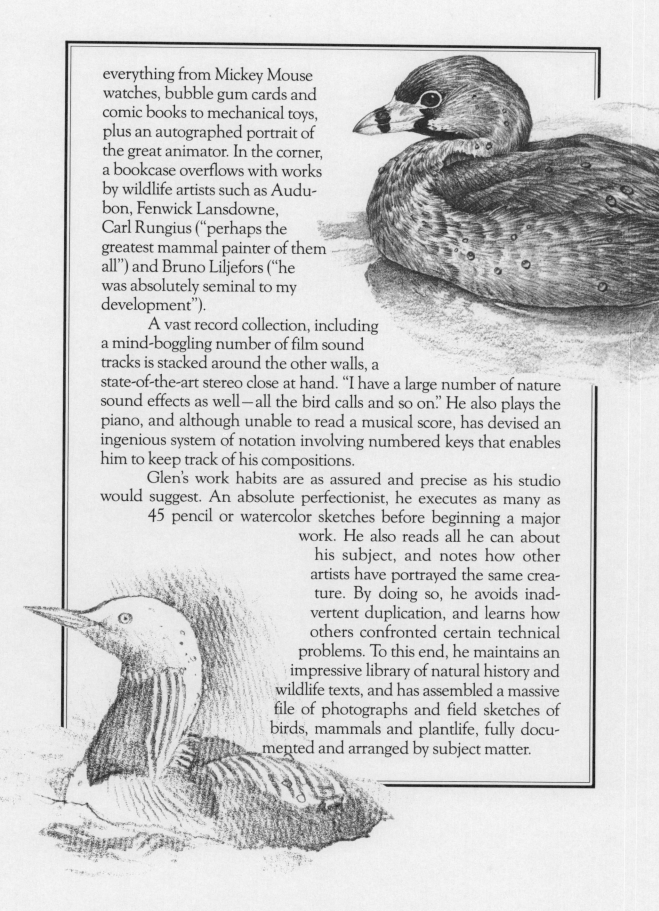

everything from Mickey Mouse watches, bubble gum cards and comic books to mechanical toys, plus an autographed portrait of the great animator. In the corner, a bookcase overflows with works by wildlife artists such as Audubon, Fenwick Lansdowne, Carl Rungius ("perhaps the greatest mammal painter of them all") and Bruno Liljefors ("he was absolutely seminal to my development").

A vast record collection, including a mind-boggling number of film sound tracks is stacked around the other walls, a state-of-the-art stereo close at hand. "I have a large number of nature sound effects as well—all the bird calls and so on." He also plays the piano, and although unable to read a musical score, has devised an ingenious system of notation involving numbered keys that enables him to keep track of his compositions.

Glen's work habits are as assured and precise as his studio would suggest. An absolute perfectionist, he executes as many as 45 pencil or watercolor sketches before beginning a major work. He also reads all he can about his subject, and notes how other artists have portrayed the same creature. By doing so, he avoids inadvertent duplication, and learns how others confronted certain technical problems. To this end, he maintains an impressive library of natural history and wildlife texts, and has assembled a massive file of photographs and field sketches of birds, mammals and plantlife, fully documented and arranged by subject matter.

Photographs are important aids which enable Glen to double-check the details of an animal's anatomy, the sequence of its actions and subtleties of its movement. But even the finest photograph remains no substitute for direct experience. "I use them only for reference," he says. "I think my field sketches contain a far greater level of observation and amount of information. Also, photos aren't a reliable color guide. There are too many variants: the type of film, the lighting conditions or poor quality reproduction." This is why he prefers to verify his sketches by borrowing stuffed specimens or skins from the Royal Ontario Museum, although even these have their drawbacks: "They're useful for checking the size, shape and arrangement of, say, a bird's feathers. But they have a stiff, unnatural look, and the beak and talons discolor very shortly after death." In all, Glen continues to rely on the colorations he obtains himself from live specimens in the wild, at zoos, or at one of several nature preserves.

A typical painting begins with a review of his field sketches, spread out on a work table. From these, Glen selects one or two which seem to him the most dramatic and characteristic. At this stage, he often makes a number of watercolor roughs, using bold slashes of wash to check the balance of his composition and experiment with color placement.

Then, using the sketches as a guide, he makes one or more highly detailed pencil renderings, working directly on watercolor paper. This stage may continue for several days, until he arrives at a satisfactory composition. *The Bald Eagle*, for example, was developed through a sequence of very different studies, from a rear view with wings lowered and head turned back toward the viewer, to a full frontal treatment with wings outstretched.

Because he is left-handed, Glen must guard against a natural tendency to position his subjects with the dominant portion of their anatomy towards the left side of the paper. To avoid this, he sometimes makes his final pencil drawing on onionskin transfer paper, then presses it against a watercolor sheet to obtain a mirror image, over which the finished painting is made. In any case, the final drawings are executed with great precision, usually with the aid of

museum samples, reference photographs, and tools such as rulers, calipers and proportional dividers.

Most of Glen's paintings are done on hand-made Fabriano watercolor paper, imported from Italy. He finds it far less absorbent than commercially manufactured stock, with the result that paints remain on the surface and retain their richness. Larger compositions are executed on custom-made American etching paper or gesso-treated linen stretched on a wooden frame.

Glen begins each painting with details of the subject's eyes and head. When these have been completed, he evaluates the work and decides whether or not to proceed: "If the facial expression doesn't have the right feel, there's no sense in going on, so I tear it up and start again. I'm my own worst critic, my own worst enemy, really. If I'm dissatisfied at *any* point, I'll scrap the whole thing. *I* have to be happy with something if others are to accept it."

Colors are mixed from Winsor & Newton pigments, then applied in a series of broad, loose strokes. Glen starts with light washes before overpainting in progressively darker hues to give certain areas a three-dimensional effect. Next comes the fine detail— the intricate textures of fur and feather, worked up with a small sable brush.

Highlights may be added with Chinese white, a special drawing ink. Most watercolorists suggest highlights by scraping away the paint with a knife, or by leaving an area unpainted altogether, counting on white paper to indicate the sheen of an animal's fur or the glint in its eye. Opaque paints and inks are frowned upon by orthodox practitioners, but Glen disagrees: "After a great deal of experimentation, I found that I could use these inks and other unconventional materials to achieve precisely the effects I want, effects that are impossible to create with watercolors alone. I see no reason why I shouldn't use them, if they're uniquely capable of doing the job."

By working almost exclusively in watercolor, Glen perpetuates the legacy of Audubon, Fuertes and Thorburn. His allegiance to this medium stems also from his admiration for his contemporaries Fenwick Lansdowne and Roger Tory Peterson, bird painters who

Great blue Heron

GLEN
LOATES

work primarily in watercolor. Over the years, Glen has experimented with oils and acrylics, drawing inks and chalk pastels, but has always returned to watercolor as the medium best suited to rendering the detail, brilliance and life-like appearance his style demands. In addition, its portability makes it ideal for working out-of-doors.

But no medium serves to accelerate the pace. Glen will often spend two to three months on a single painting. As a result, he seldom produces more than three or four major works a year, along with a dozen or so smaller treatments and watercolor sketches. Many larger works are commissioned by clients, who specify a painting's subject matter. While Glen welcomes such assignments (excluding only hunters who want him to portray their kills), these constant requests impose a limitation. "I have a great number of ideas for future paintings," he says. "I'd like to get back to insects and underwater life, but I never seem to have the time. The nicest commission is from the person who says: paint what you want. But, as I've said, I won't paint something I haven't seen. Also, unlike many other artists who have several paintings on the go at once, I find I can concentrate on only one picture at a time."

Another peril of commissioned work is that the client may, consciously or otherwise, attempt to dictate the tone and content of the work. This, of course, is totally contrary to Glen's beliefs. His subjects live their lives independent of the human observer, in no sense "posing" for the artist. Nothing is exaggerated or hyperbolized; nothing caters to a human sensibility.

Lesser animal painters have found they can make their work more marketable by emphasizing a predator's ferocity, or by portraying small, furry creatures in a manner that can only be described as cloying and "cute." Anthropomorphism—the attribution of human characteristics to an animal—is a contentious issue in the field of wildlife art, and one that must be examined in some detail to appreciate Glen's unique approach.

Glen never attempts to depict his animals in a way that conforms to stereotypical ideals. Cuteness is not overblown; violence remains unglorified. His predators are immune from moral judgement: the golden eagle kills a snowshoe rabbit simply because that is what it, in fact, does. "A predator is *equipped* to kill," Glen says. "Brutality is inherent in nature. Certainly I'll depict that moment, because it appeals to me on the bases of composition and power. Technically, it can involve the greater challenge, but I'm in no sense distorting or misrepresenting the facts. The moment exists, and I simply capture it as best I can."

On the other hand, Glen believes it impossible for a sensitive artist *not* to inject emotion into his work: "I try to paint my subjects sympathetically, not sentimentally. But it's hard to paint rabbits, bear cubs and chipmunks that *aren't* cute. Have you ever seen fox pups? They look like they've just come out of the dryer. They're fluffy and adorable, you can't deny it, and you'd be wrong if you tried. Humans aren't unique in their emotions, instincts and curiosities, so it's quite natural for wildlife artists to depict an animal that displays human-like characteristics."

As well, Glen has noticed that his paintings of raccoons, bears, foxes, rabbits and fawns are especially popular with small children, and he derives a great deal of pleasure from talking with them about his work. "It's deeply gratifying for me to see how kids respond to my pictures," he says. "I'm sure Walt Disney must have felt the same sense of satisfaction when he saw how children reacted to his cartoon characters; I know *I* thought they were a fairy tale come to life. Kids today are much more practical, but that's simply another dimension, and it's terrific. They're remarkably well attuned to environmental issues; they'll come up to me at shows and tell me that they hope my pictures will help save the little animals. Believe me, that's a great inspiration to keep on painting."

Although Glen takes pride in his ability to portray nature in a highly convincing manner (a visitor to an exhibition of his work once tried to brush a painted mosquito off one of the flower studies), he stresses that his main objective is to create art, not well-framed pages from a biology text. "An animal painting is much more than a detailed study of feathers or fur," he says. "This was the great lesson Fuertes taught: there's a balance between accuracy and aesthetics. A lot of artists get so carried away with detail that they painstakingly paint in every hair of a mammal's coat, all the little

Bald Eagle with ♀ Mallard

Neck feather pattern

♂ Mallards

lines and barbs on a bird's feathers. That won't work. It's lifeless and devoid of feeling. It's also inaccurate, because these details are only discernable on the part of the animal closest to the viewer; the rest of the body appears flat or shaded, due to its contours and a natural foreshortening.

"On the other hand, I've always thought it a cop-out to suggest movement with a few sweeping brush strokes. That's cheating the viewer. If an artist is capable of rendering the finest detail on select parts of the animal's anatomy, he'll achieve a better likeness, suggesting power and movement in a more realistic manner."

Detail aside, another hallmark of Glen's paintings is mood, an elusive quality suggested by the atmosphere enveloping his subjects—weather, clouds, a hint of moisture in the air, and seasonal changes—or by the manner in which he poses an animal. Often he may intentionally restrain the atmosphere, creating the sense of surprise or awe that one experiences when suddenly coming upon a creature normally glimpsed only at a distance. With this approach, Glen pays homage to Archibald Thorburn, by turning his subjects toward the viewer for maximum impact and intimacy, as in *Blue Jay* and *Timber Wolves*.

Additional evidence of Glen's former mentors is difficult to detect in his most recent work. Glen's present style is very much his own. The lessons that his masters taught were learned 30 years ago and more; now nature is his only teacher.

Nevertheless, he views each new project as an important learning experience: "Because I'm essentially self-taught, I've never been afraid to experiment and accept new challenges with every painting I create. I'm constantly striving to improve my technical skills, and I feel I still have a great deal more to learn about interpreting nature on paper. I think I'm more selective now, better able to exercise control. In the early days, *everything* was exciting to paint. It's very difficult to pare down, to discriminate and economize.

"I think I've managed to set certain standards. I think the body of work I've done would be enough for others to gain something, to take it one step further. And I'm sure somebody will. Nobody is the best; I certainly don't think *I'm* the best. The concept

is subjective and meaningless, the work has to speak for itself. It's up to the public to accept or reject any artist; *they'll* decide who's the best in their eyes. I do what I do to the best of my abilities, and that's all anybody can say. Surely that's enough."

And what of the future? Glen Loates is aware in his mind of where he wants to go, in terms of new ideas and approaches as yet unrealized. The results will be interesting indeed.

His only regret is that he cannot devote more time to environmental issues. He believes that the popularity of his art is inextricably bound up with the public's concern for endangered species and what he calls a "raised ecological consciousness."

"I've taken more from nature than I can ever give in return," he says. "I owe so much, having painted all these beautiful things. If I can assist in the preservation of natural areas by lending my name to conservation projects, or by using my art to draw attention to environmental issues, I feel I'm repaying an enormous debt of gratitude. There are so few unspoiled areas left in the world. Society is upsetting a delicate balance, threatening the very existence of so much wildlife. I hope that in some small way my work will make people cherish wild animals, and preserve the areas that survive intact."

This is Glen Loates' most fervent hope. And no one who sees the magnificent art reproduced on these pages would want to do anything less.

GLEN LOATES

PLATES & COMMENTARY

Jug Study #1

Jug Study #2

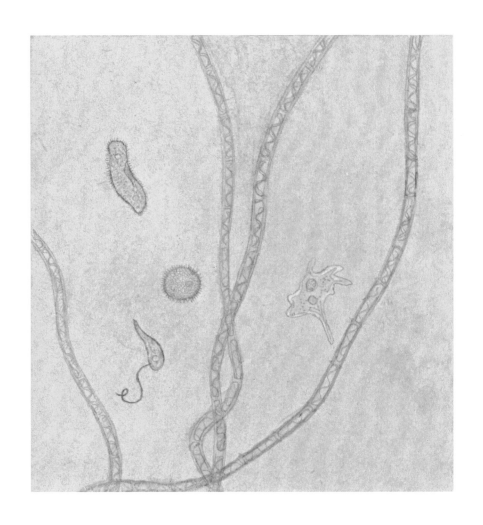

Swamp Life

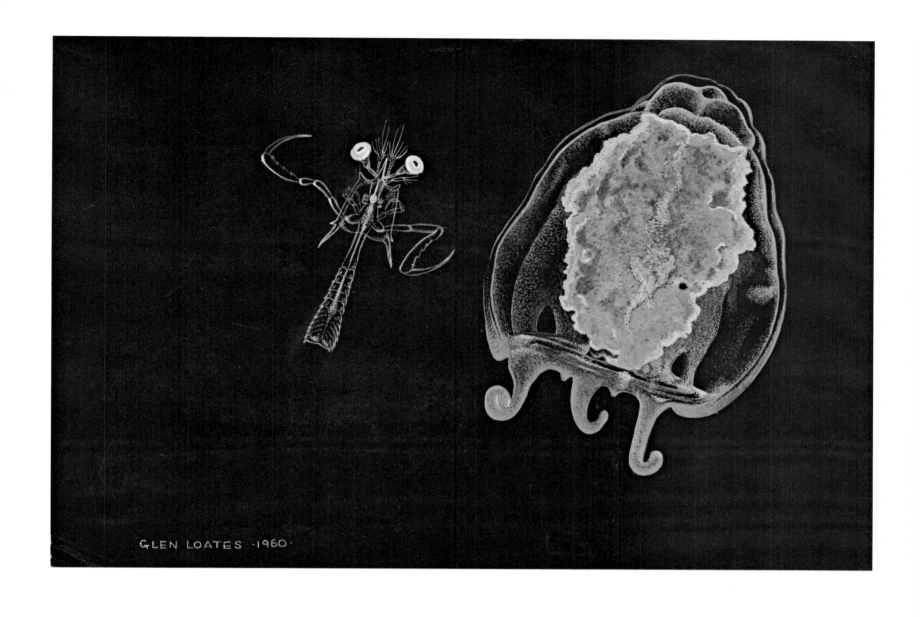

GLEN LOATES ·1960·

*Artists, as they develop their skills over
the years, experiment with various painting techniques to
achieve a given result. During the early part of
my career, I chose to concentrate on a scene where the main
subject was highlighted while the surrounding
foreground and background was subdued. This approach
is obvious in the painting of the Pickerel Weed.
The plant is the main subject while its surroundings are
indicated with a soft wash. I have introduced
a colorful dragonfly and water droplets to suggest the
plants' shoreline habitat.*

Pickerel Weed

Shooting Stars

LOATES 1964

Hawkweed

*The beauty of our wild flowers has
always fascinated me. As a young boy I would frequently
explore the rolling hills of the Don Valley.
I can vividly recall the lush carpet of purple violets on
the woodland floor each spring and swaying
fields of black-eyed susans during the summer months and
then the splendid splash of color of the wild
hawkweed and corn flower heralding the coming fall.*

Trillium

Corn Flower

Black Eyed Susan

Wild Columbine

Wild Rose

M. G. LOATES

Polar Bear

The Aristocrat

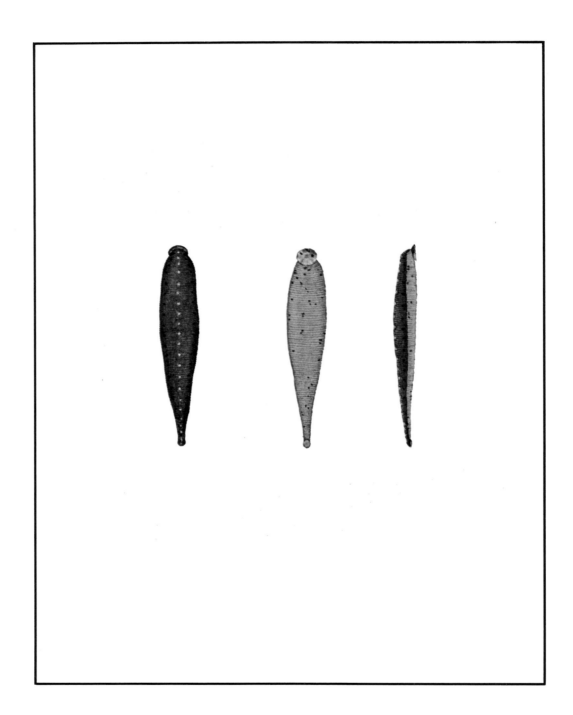

Pond Leech Study

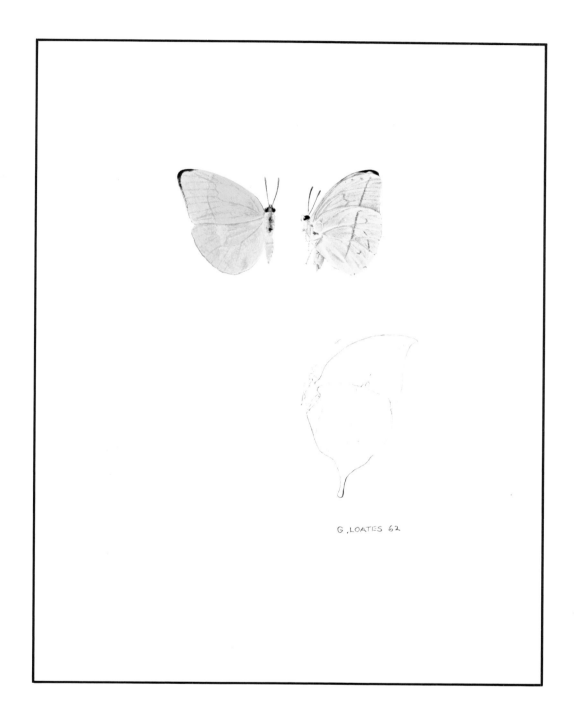

G .LOATES 62

Butterfly Study

Animated Cartoon Preliminary #1

Animated Cartoon Preliminary #2

Golden Crowned Kinglets

Yellow Warbler

Blue Jays

The blue jay is undoubtedly one of my favorite birds. An annual resident in many parts of eastern North America, it is perhaps the most resourceful of our native birds. With a showy flash of blue, white and black plumage, blue jays maintain their high spirits against the harshest conditions of the winter months. It is only during the early spring, the time of nesting, that we hardly ever see any of these frisky birds. Their stout twig nests are generally well-camouflaged in evergreens, or perhaps — as in my painting — in the crotch of a heavily-leafed maple tree.

Following page:
Ring-Necked Pheasant

D. LOATES 1965

White Trilliums

Painted Trilliums

White Trilliums

Purple Violets

Queen Anne's Lace

Opposite: Grizzly Bear (Detail)

Grizzly Bear
There was a time during the early 1960s when I felt it was necessary to
depict my subject with a full or completely painted background. On reflection, I feel I
was attempting to create a visual happening or awareness in the viewer that the
main subject was real in every sense of the word: not just a museum mount or a natural
history exhibit but reality in everyday life. My subject could have been
blue jays nesting in a maple, or a chance meeting of grizzly bears in some remote
British Columbian mountain gorge; there was this urge to make it real, to push it
beyond a merely scientific illustration. It wasn't long before I realised I was defeating my
purpose. The background setting was too elaborate and the main image was
secondary. In my mind, I was simply becoming a landscape artist. After vigorous
experimentation I have found it is possible to introduce backgrounds in a more
subtle manner without an overwhelming effect.

Saw-Whet Owl (Detail)

Opposite: Saw-Whet Owl,
To thousands of bird-watchers throughout eastern North America,
the saw-whet owl brings one of the most welcome of all night sounds, with the suggestion
of the mystery of darkness and the sweep of soft-feathered wings
from tree to tree while other birds are soundless and asleep.
Saw-Whet owls are little fellows, somewhat shorter than robins but normally
appearing much stouter because of their big round heads, stubby
tails and rather loose, soft feathers. Like other birds of prey, they are meat eaters,
living largely on mice, large insects such as grasshoppers, cicadas and
night-flying moths, and a scattering of miscellaneous small creatures. They are
definitely beneficial to mankind through their destruction of crop pests, as indeed are
practically all of our owls and hawks.
You could hardly ask for a more friendly bird. In the days when country and
suburban houses were ornamented with filigreed copings and cornices,
Saw-Whet owls often slept among the recesses during the day and even nested there.
Old orchards and ancient shade trees around houses are still favorite homesites,
for here the birds are likely to find the sort of limb cavities they prefer as hiding places
for the four or five eggs that the female lays sometime in April or early May.

Monarch Chrysalid

Opposite: Plant Study

G. LOATES - 1977 -

Presenting my limited edition book to Prime Minister Pierre E. Trudeau,
accompanied by my brother Bernard.

Opposite: Canada Warbler

Following pages:

Pumpkin Patch

Common Crows

Opposite: Eastern Chipmunk

*As it dashes through the shrubbery or along a stone wall, the
chipmunk always takes time to stop and satisfy itself about passers-by. A pair of bright
eyes in the sharp little face look out with mingled shyness and
curiosity. The rusty coat is decorated with black and white stripes, but a pastel
quality dispels any suggestion of garishness. In spite of its inquisitiveness, it seldom
intrudes and is easily frightened away if it does.*

*The chipmunk wants plenty of food, and wants it handy. During the fall it collects
provisions for the winter. It crams the food into its mouth pouches,
filling them until its cheeks and the sides of its neck bulge like those of a child with the mumps.
After biting any sharp projections, for instance the dried
calyx stem from the hickory nut, the chipmunk tucks the objects into its mouth, using its hands
dexterously and filling each cheek alternately until the load is evenly balanced.
Then it scampers off to its burrow.
It piles enough provisions under its bed to raise it to the ceiling. In exceptional cases a
chipmunk may collect a half-bushel of nuts and grains.
Throughout the cold winter it doesn't have to get out of its warm bed for meals: it can
just reach down under the covers. As the winter wears on and the
chipmunk continues to draw from this pantry, the bed slowly sinks down from the ceiling
and by spring it has reached the floor.
Because chipmunks can depend upon their stores of food, they do not fatten up as squirrels do.*

Fawn (Study)

Opposite: Fawn

M. G. LOATES

Lesser Scaup (Study)

Opposite: Lesser Scaup

GLEN
LOATES

LESSER SCAUP ♀ ♂

Key Deer (Pewter Sculpture)

Cougar (Pewter Sculpture)

Timber Wolf (Pewter Sculpture)

Grizzly Bear (Pewter Sculpture)

Red-Headed Woodpecker (Study)

Opposite: Red-Headed Woodpecker

Harlequin Duck
The Harlequin Duck can be found on both coasts of North America. The showily-marked male is quite a contrast to his smaller, dusky brown mate.

My attention was first drawn to these delightful birds while visiting the coast of British Columbia. I watched with fascination as they floated high on the surface of a rolling wave, only to disappear as another wave came to a crest, hiding them from sight momentarily. I watched with binoculars, taking notes from behind the protection of the west coast rocky shores. Occasionally I would be sprayed by a breaker as it rolled in, smashing against the rocks. I was most impressed by the endurance of the wonderful little ducks in the stormy weather. The experience of observing their behavior and beauty is one I shall always savor.

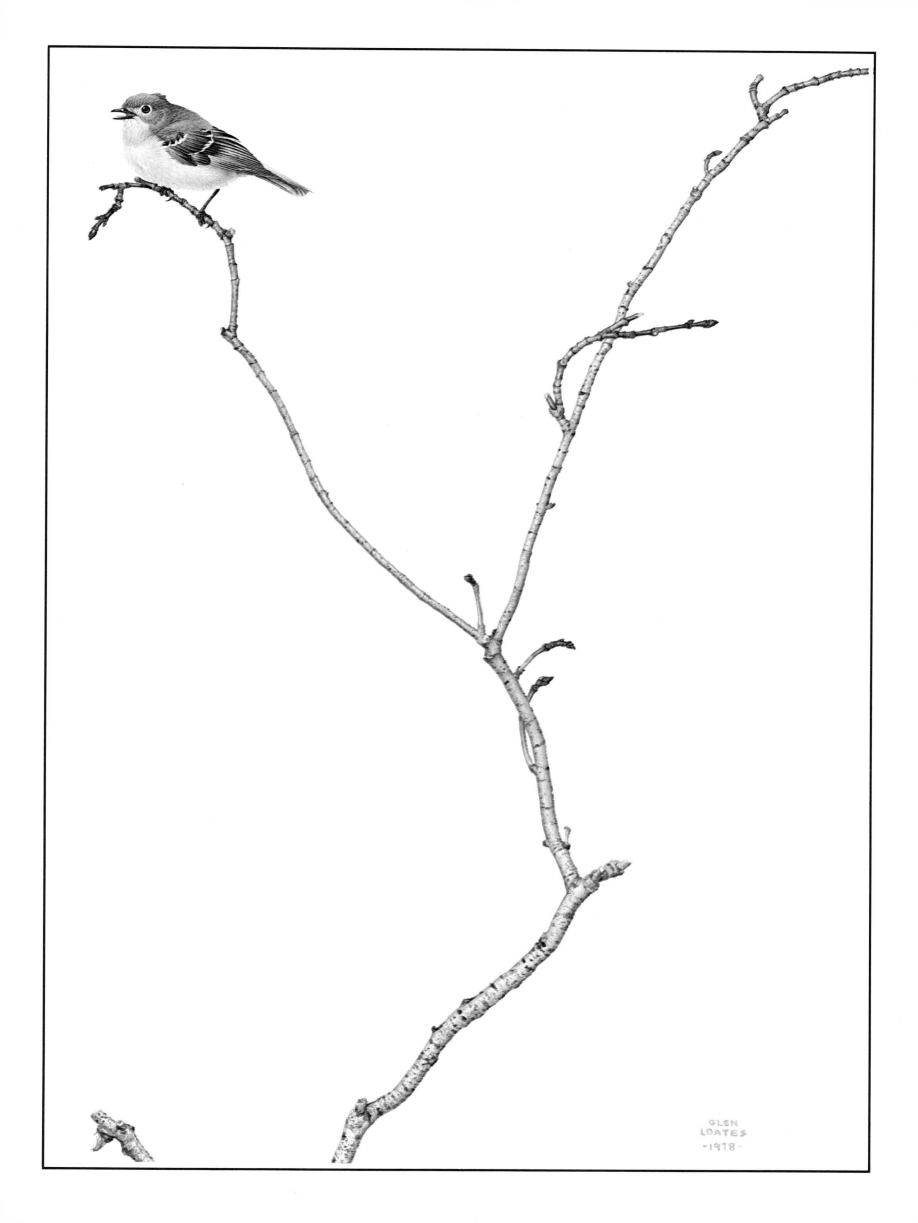

GLEN
LOATES
-1978-

An Autumn Day
Those of us who
live in the temperate regions
experience remarkable
changes in the weather
with the passage of
the seasons.

Opposite: Magnolia Warbler

Following Pages:

Downy Woodpecker

Western Magpie

Chickadees (Detail)

Opposite: Chickadees
Anyone living in the eastern region of North America has heard the
song after which this little bird is named. So friendly and so common a winter visitor, it has
been depicted in school texts, nature movies and even animated features.
Primarily a woodland species, the black-capped chickadee roams in noisy flocks of three
or more birds. Their food consists of insects and their larvae,
berries, seeds and various fruits. They nest in evacuated woodpecker holes, natural
cavities or holes made in rotten trees. Normally the nest contains six to eight
eggs which are white with a dusting of brown.
The black-capped chickadee is easily baited to outdoor feeding stations with suet
or sunflower seeds.

Opposite: Blue Jay
These are the only jays found over most of the settled parts of
eastern North America. Most of those living in Canada migrate south, but a number of
these strikingly beautiful birds remain in their breeding areas throughout the winter.
Although birds of the forest, they have adapted well to human presence, and are readily
attracted to feeding stations; at times they even nest in city gardens and ravines.
Their diet consists of almost anything edible, plant or animal. Although they consume snails,
eggs, frogs, mice and birds, most of the animal material they eat consists of insects
including such pests as beetles, grasshoppers, caterpillars and weevils. However, grains, wild
berries, nuts and fruit of almost any type comprise nearly three quarters of their food.
Although blue jays prefer to live in mixed forests, they build their nests most
often on branches in dense coniferous thickets. Sticks, leaves, bark and grass form the raw
materials of these nests, which are lined with fine rootlets. The eggs are generally
an olive buff color, with small spots of dull brown scattered evenly over the surface.

Cedar Waxwings
Anyone who has travelled in or visited mid-North America would be acquainted with our best-dressed bird. Cedar waxwings with their brown crests and black-eyed masks, are likely to be seen in groups, perhaps in a row on a branch passing some choice bit of food from one to another. I had observed the birds in my painting resting after eating a feast of flies in the Georgian Bay area.

Following Pages:
Cardinals

Cooper's Hawk

GLEN
LOATES
-1981-

Whitetail Deer (Field Sketch)

Opposite: Whitetail Deer
Standing straight up, the white tails of these deer flash
signals of alarm as they whisk through the woods. No other big game in
North America is as widely-known and hunted as the whitetail deer.
As with all male deer, the buck's principal accomplishment during the summer is
the growing of a new set of antlers. These decorative weapons start in April
or May as a couple of bulbous swellings, just in front of his ears. Covered with skin
or "velvet" through which courses a multitude of blood vessels, the antlers
grow rapidly. The owner is very careful with them, for they are now soft and sensitive.
Any real injury to them at this stage results in a permanent mark or
deformity. If cut, they bleed freely like any other part of the body. Once the antlers are
clean and polished, the buck's disposition alters markedly.
No longer is he retiring, content to live on perhaps one hundred acres of land. His neck
enlarges, becoming twice its normal size. He stalks boldly through
the woods looking for mates.
In 1967 I observed these beautiful mammals and drew many sketches of them running
across an open field and leaping over a split-rail fence. The drawings
were completely forgotten until the early 1970's when I purchased a copy of a sports
magazine with a painting of whitetail deer on the cover which brought
to mind my earlier experience. With this reference and other photographic material I
developed a somewhat finished drawing that appears in my first book.
Then in 1983 I came across another group of whitetails running into the woods and was
inspired to complete the painting.

Canada Lynx (Detail)

Opposite: Canada Lynx

The lynx is usually a silent animal. Even when caught in a trap,
except for possible hissing and spitting, it may remain stoical to the end. Occasionally it and its
companions will call back and forth while hunting together, but many naturalists and hunters with years of
experience in the woods have heard the low catlike "me-eow" only once or twice. However,
at mating time, late in winter, the lynx may let loose a series of yells
that compensate for a whole year of restraint. Two males will shout at each other in tones that probably cause
the mice and other small animals to shudder in their snow-bound burrows!
The lynx looks like an over-grown tabby cat with high-tufted ears
and a dignified ruff. It has long legs, very big feet, and a ridiculously short tail. It lives only in the northern
coniferous forests and adjacent tundra where the winter cold is long and intense. The soft winter coat
which keeps the lynx warm on long hunting trips is pastel-shaded gray fur sprinkled with a faint brown. In some
lights it has a lavender tint. More than 2.5 cms (1 inch) thick, the coat
is made of hair up to 10 cms (4 inches) long. In summer it is more brownish and of course is lighter weight.
Because the lynx is shy and essentially a night-prowler, few people ever
see it. Those fortunate enough are most impressed by its penetrating eyes. In daylight the pupils of its eyes
are reduced to the tightest slits; the yellow irises seem to cover the entire eyeballs.
Throughout most of its range, the lynx is able to stay in the deep woods.
There on the log-littered forest floor it hunts as silently as a shadow. Depending on circumstances, the
lynx may still-hunt or lie in wait for a passing victim. If game is abundant, it may climb on a ledge,
a fallen log, or an overhanging tree from which it can leap down on its prey. Usually
it moves slowly, crouching down to be as inconspicuous as possible. From
time to time, as it reaches a log or just below a ridge crest, it gradually straightens up to full height
for a long, careful scrutiny of the terrain ahead.

© GLEN
LOATES
-1983-

Golden Eagle (Detail)

Following Pages: Golden Eagle
With a wingspan of over 2 metres (7 feet) the golden eagle is the largest
of our native eagles. It ranges over more than half of the world's land masses, preferring
canyons, mountainous or hilly terrain with large tracts of open spaces for
hunting. Its diet consists mainly of small mammals and birds such as squirrels, ground hogs,
rabbits, ducks, pheasant, grouse and other large birds. Prey as large as deer
and sheep have also been successfully taken.
The golden eagle's aerie is generally found on the edge of a cliff
commanding a wide expanse of territory. The nest containing two or three whitish eggs is
constructed of a mass of material made up from various sticks and lined
with moss. The name 'golden eagle' is derived from the golden appearance of the head
feathers and those around its neck. (The young have white tails with a broad,
sharply defined black terminal band.)
There is nothing quite as unforgettable as the eerie, high pitched screech of
this magnificent bird echoing its way along the canyons of remote northern landscapes.

The following pages are preliminary renderings and working drawings for Bald Eagle.

© GLEN
LOATES
-1982-

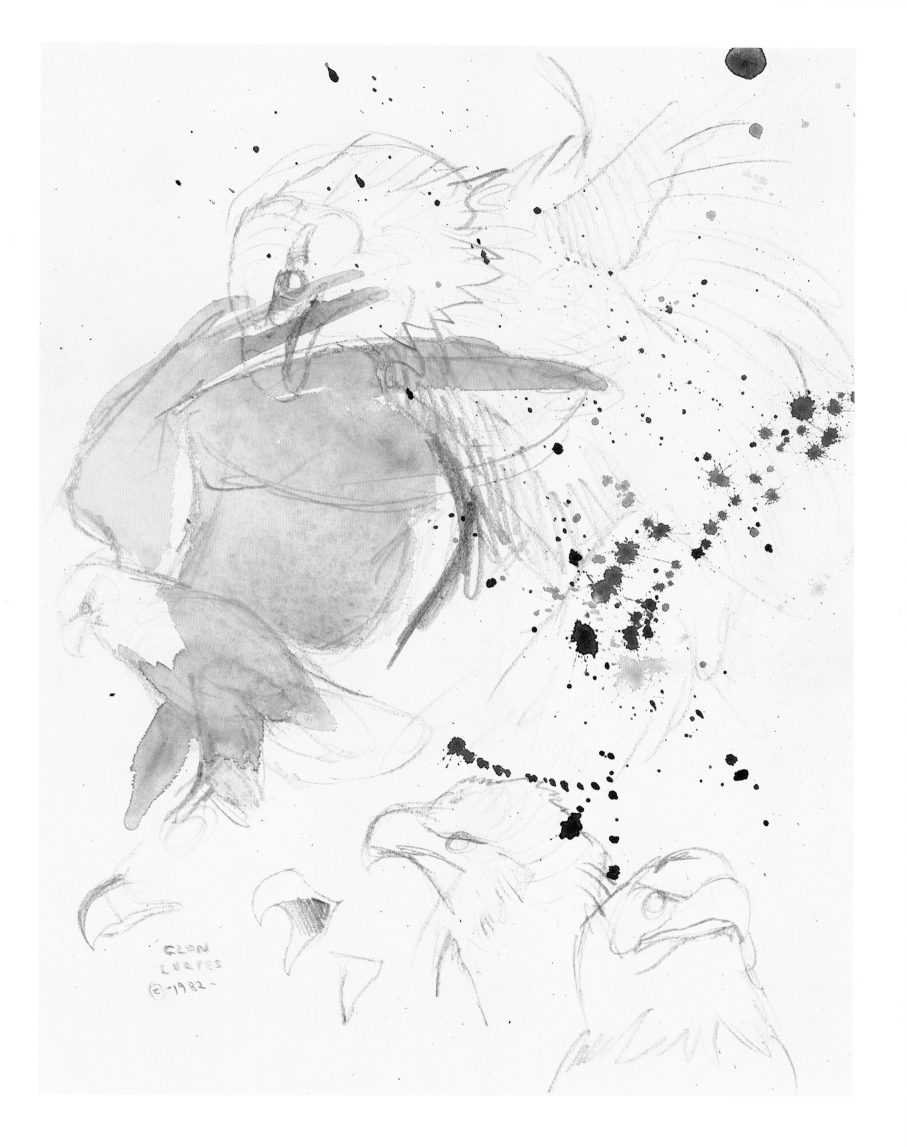

GLEN
LOATES
© -1982-

© GLEN
LOATES
-1982-

Bald Eagle

July 4, 1776—America's first Independence Day: the Continental Congress wanted a brand new seal, or symbol, to go with its brand new nation. Benjamin Franklin, John Adams, and Thomas Jefferson were picked to come up with the design. An easy job for three great men, right? Wrong! Four years and dozens of ideas later, the U.S. still had no official seal.

A second committee tried again in 1780. No luck. A third met in May of 1782. But still nothing looked right. Then the problem was handed to the Secretary of Congress, Charles Thompson. In just one week, he came up with a winner. From the first committee, Mr. Thompson took the ideas of a shield, a scroll, and a Latin Motto, E Pluribus Unum (Out of Many, One). From the second committee he picked 13 stripes, 13 stars, an olive branch, and an arrow. From the third group came a small eagle, the ancient symbol of strength and power. The eagle was the idea of William Barton, an artist picked by the committee to design the seal. But eagles had appeared on other nations' seals. Mr. Thompson wanted his seal to be strictly American. He decided to use a bald eagle. It lived on no other continent.

Mr. Thompson sketched out his ideas: A section of blue on the red-and-white shield; a circle of clouds around the stars; an olive branch for peace in the eagle's right claw; arrows for war in its left. Then he took his drawing (which looked like a chicken in a thunderstorm) back to William Barton for more work. Together the two men came up with a design that Congress really loved. Approval was voted for the Great Seal on June 20, 1782. The bald eagle was the new symbol of the United States of America. It was now the "official" eagle!

Bald Eagle

© GLEN
LOATES
1982

Bald Eagle

© GLEN LORTSS

*Presenting Bald Eagle to President Ronald Reagan on behalf of the
Canadian people to the American people during the Year of the Eagle. My brother Bernard
and the Canadian Ambassador Allan Gotlieb accompanied me.*

Following pages:

Goshawk

Rough-Legged Hawk

Marsh Hawk

41/105   m. c. l...

41/125

Great Horned Owl

Most any small animal or bird which
moves may be seized by this
big nocturnal hunter.
Even skunks and porcupines may
sometimes be attacked.
So the stately looking wise old owl
is probably not so wise at all,
and certainly has no sense of smell.

Following pages:

Saw-Whet Owl

Gray Jay

Common Raven

White-Breasted Nuthatch

Red-Breasted Nuthatch

Winter Wren

Golden-Crowned Kinglet

Ruby-Crowned Kinglet

Bohemian Waxwing

Starling

41/125

41/125   m.g. lot...

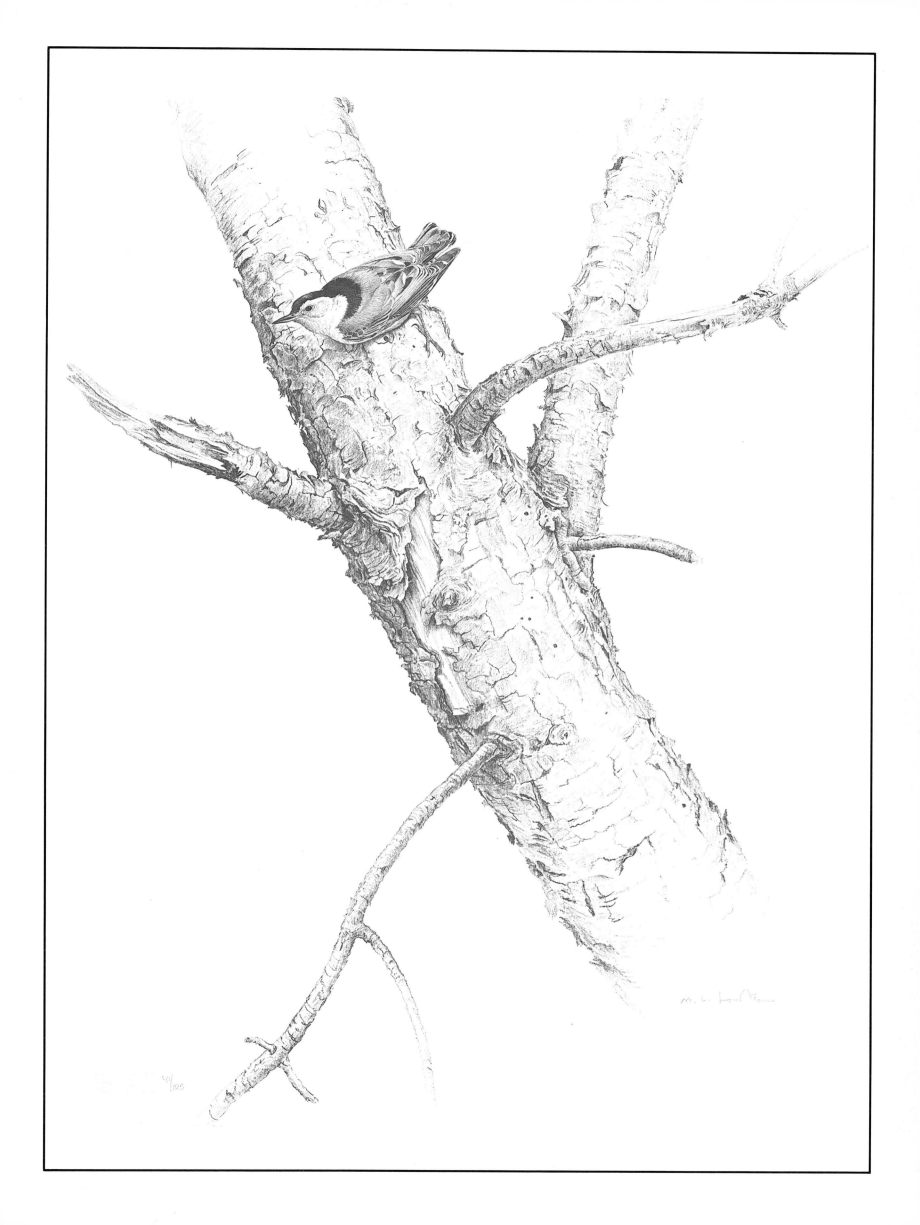

44/100

41/85